KARMA YOGA & PREM YOGA

Swami Vivekananda

Pharos Books

ISBN: 978-93-6700-183-7

©Publishers
Publisher: Pharos Books (P) Ltd.
Plot No.-63, 1st Floor, Main Mother Dairy Road
Pandav Nagar, East Delhi-110092
Phone: +14049995474, 011-40395855
WhatsApp: +91 9319228272
E-mail: sales@pharosbooks.in
Website: www.pharosbooks.in

Edition: 2025

Printed By: Sushma Book Binding House, Okhla
Industrial Area, Phase II, New Delhi-110020

Karma-Yoga and Prem-Yoga
By : Swami Vivekananda

Swami Vivekananda

Swami Vivekananda (1863-1902), born as Narendranath Datta in Kolkata, India, is revered as one of India's most influential spiritual leaders and a key figure in the introduction of Indian philosophies of Vedanta and Yoga to the Western world. A disciple of the saint Ramakrishna Paramahamsa, Swami Vivekananda played a crucial role in reviving Hinduism, advocating for social reforms, and fostering interfaith harmony. His legacy is far-reaching, touching upon religion, spirituality, education, and nationalism, and his thoughts continue to inspire people across the globe.

Early Life and Education

Born on January 12, 1863, into a well-educated and aristocratic Bengali family, Narendranath showed signs of intellectual brilliance and deep spirituality from an early age. His father, Vishwanath Datta, was a successful attorney with a progressive outlook, while his mother, Bhuvaneshwari Devi, was deeply religious and instilled in him strong moral values and devotion to the divine. Vivekananda's inquisitive nature led him to study a wide range of subjects, from Western philosophy and history to Sanskrit scriptures. He was particularly influenced by the works of the English poet William Wordsworth and the writings of Ralph Waldo Emerson, John Stuart Mill, and Herbert Spencer.

However, his search for spiritual truth went beyond academic learning. Vivekananda was deeply troubled by the social inequalities, poverty, and religious dogmatism in India. His spiritual quest led him to Ramakrishna, a mystic and saint from Dakshineswar, whose teachings would change the course of his life.

Association with Ramakrishna

Vivekananda's meeting with Ramakrishna in 1881 marked the beginning of a transformative spiritual journey. Ramakrishna taught him that all religions lead to the same ultimate truth and that service to humanity was the greatest form of worship. Under his guidance, Vivekananda learned about Advaita Vedanta, which emphasizes the oneness of the soul (Atman) and the Divine (Brahman). After Ramakrishna's death in 1886, Vivekananda, along with his fellow disciples, established the Ramakrishna Order, dedicated to serving humanity and spreading the spiritual wisdom of their master.

Spiritual Wanderer and the Chicago Parliament of Religions

After renouncing worldly life, Vivekananda travelled across India as a wandering monk between 1888 and 1893. His travels exposed him to the plight of the poor and the deep spiritual hunger of the Indian masses. This experience shaped his vision of social service and spiritual upliftment, reinforcing his belief that the alleviation of poverty and ignorance was essential for India's resurgence.

In 1893, Vivekananda travelled to the United States, where he delivered a historic speech at the Parliament of the World's Religions in Chicago. His opening words, "Sisters and Brothers of America," and his message of universal brotherhood and tolerance for all religions received a standing ovation and established him as an eloquent spokesperson for India's spiritual heritage. He introduced the Western world to the principles of Vedanta and Yoga, emphasizing the idea of the essential unity of all beings, transcending religious and cultural differences.

Teachings and Philosophy

Vivekananda's teachings centred on the principles of Vedanta and the practice of Yoga, emphasizing the divinity of the soul, the oneness of existence, and the potential of human beings to attain spiritual enlightenment. He believed in the harmonious coexistence of science and religion, viewing them as complementary paths to understanding the ultimate reality. His philosophy was not confined to metaphysical ideas but extended to practical spirituality, where he encouraged individuals to serve society selflessly, upholding the idea of "Jiva is Shiva" – every human being is a manifestation of the divine.

He was also a strong advocate for education, considering it the key to social transformation. He believed that education should not only focus on intellectual development but also on character building and the realization of one's inner strength. For Vivekananda, the empowerment of the masses, especially women and the underprivileged, was essential for India's progress.

Contribution to Indian Nationalism and Social Reform

Swami Vivekananda is often hailed as a pioneer of Indian nationalism. His vision of India was rooted in a spiritual foundation, where religious unity would lead to social and political strength. He sought to awaken the Indian youth to their immense potential, urging them to embrace fearlessness, self-reliance, and moral integrity. His famous call, "Arise, awake, and stop not until the goal is reached," continues to resonate as a powerful message of self-empowerment and national pride.

Vivekananda was also a social reformer who criticized the rigid caste system, gender discrimination, and religious intolerance. He believed that India's rejuvenation would come through the upliftment of the downtrodden and the dismantling of oppressive social structures. His emphasis on karma yoga, or selfless service, laid the groundwork for future social and political movements in India, including the Indian independence struggle.

Establishment of the Ramakrishna Mission

In 1897, Vivekananda founded the Ramakrishna Mission, an organization dedicated to social service, education, and spiritual development. The Mission continues to operate schools, hospitals, and charitable institutions worldwide, reflecting Vivekananda's belief in the importance of combining spiritual knowledge with practical action. The Ramakrishna Mission remains a living embodiment of his philosophy of serving humanity as a path to self-realization.

Legacy and Influence

Swami Vivekananda passed away at the young age of 39 on July 4, 1902, but his legacy endures. His teachings have influenced a wide range of people, from political leaders like Mahatma Gandhi and Subhas Chandra Bose to spiritual teachers like Sri Aurobindo and Paramahansa Yogananda. In the West, his thoughts on Vedanta and Yoga shaped the intellectual discourse on spirituality, and he played a key role in the early spread of Indian spiritual practices to Europe and America.

His birthday, January 12, is celebrated as National Youth Day in India, in recognition of his enduring message to the younger generation. His words continue to inspire millions to strive for personal excellence, social justice, and spiritual enlightenment, making Swami Vivekananda a timeless figure in the global spiritual and cultural landscape.

Swami Vivekananda was much more than a spiritual leader; he was a visionary who laid the foundation for modern Indian thought, blending ancient wisdom with contemporary ideals. His emphasis on individual growth, social responsibility, and spiritual harmony continues to serve as a guiding light for generations. Through his life, teachings, and work, he not only revived the spiritual ethos of India but also gave the world a universal message of peace, unity, and compassion.

(Source : rkmath.org)

Contents

CHAPTER I
Karma in Its Effect on Character

The word Karma is derived from the Sanskrit Kri, to do; all action is Karma. Technically, this word also means the effects of actions. In connection with metaphysics, it sometimes means the effects, of which our past actions were the causes. But in Karma-Yoga we have simply to do with the word Karma as meaning work. The goal of mankind is knowledge. That is the one ideal placed before us by Eastern philosophy. Pleasure is not the goal of man, but knowledge. Pleasure and happiness come to an end. It is a mistake to suppose that pleasure is the goal. The cause of all the miseries we have in the world is that men foolishly think pleasure to be the ideal to strive for. After a time man finds that it is not happiness, but knowledge, towards which he is going, and that both pleasure and pain are great teachers, and that he learns as much from evil as from good. As pleasure and pain pass before his soul they have upon it different pictures, and the result of these combined impressions is what is called man's "character". If you take the character of any man, it really is but the aggregate of tendencies, the sum total of the bent of his mind; you will find that misery and happiness are equal factors in the formation of that character. Good and evil have an equal share in moulding character, and in some instances misery is a greater teacher than happiness. In studying the great characters the world has produced, I dare say, in the vast majority of cases, it would be found that it was misery that taught more than happiness, it was poverty that taught more than wealth, it was blows that brought out their inner fire more than praise.

Now this knowledge, again, is inherent in man. No knowledge comes from outside; it is all inside. What we say a man "knows", should, in strict psychological language, be what he "discovers" or "unveils"; what a man "learns" is really what he "discovers", by taking the cover off his own soul, which is a mine of infinite knowledge.

We say Newton discovered gravitation. Was it sitting anywhere in a corner waiting for him? It was in his own mind; the time came and he found it out. All knowledge that the world has ever received comes from the mind; the infinite library of the universe is in your own mind. The external world is simply the suggestion, the occasion, which sets you to study your own mind, but the object of your study is always your own mind. The falling of an apple gave the suggestion to Newton, and he studied his own mind. He rearranged all the previous links of thought in his mind and discovered a new link among them, which we call the law of gravitation. It was not in the apple nor in anything in the centre of the earth.

All knowledge, therefore, secular or spiritual, is in the human mind. In many cases it is not discovered, but remains covered, and when the covering is being slowly taken off, we say, "We are learning," and the advance of knowledge is made by the advance of this process of uncovering. The man from whom this veil is being lifted is the more knowing man, the man upon whom it lies thick is ignorant, and the man from whom it has entirely gone is all-knowing, omniscient. There have been omniscient men, and, I believe, there will be yet; and that there will be myriads of them in the cycles to come. Like fire in a piece of flint, knowledge exists in the mind; suggestion is the friction which brings it out. So with all our feelings and action — our tears and our smiles, our joys and our griefs, our weeping and our laughter, our curses and our blessings, our praises and our blames — every one of these we may find, if we calmly study our own selves, to have been brought out from within ourselves by so many blows. The result is what we are. All these blows taken together are called Karma — work, action. Every mental and physical blow that is given to the soul, by which, as it were, fire is struck from it, and by which its own power and knowledge are discovered, is Karma, this word being used in its widest sense. Thus we are all doing Karma all the time. I am talking to you: that is Karma. You are listening: that is Karma. We breathe: that is Karma. We walk: Karma. Everything we do, physical or mental, is Karma, and it leaves its marks on us.

There are certain works which are, as it were, the aggregate, the sum total, of a large number of smaller works. If we stand near the seashore and hear the waves dashing against the shingle, we think it is such a great noise, and yet we know that one wave is really composed of millions and millions of minute waves. Each one of these is making a noise, and yet we do not catch it; it is only when they become the big aggregate that we hear. Similarly, every pulsation of the heart is work. Certain kinds of work we feel and they become tangible to us; they are, at the same time, the aggregate of a number of small works. If you really want to judge of the character of a man, look not at his great performances. Every fool may become a hero at one time or another. Watch a man do his most common actions; those are indeed the things which will tell you the real character of a great man. Great occasions rouse even the lowest of human beings to some kind of greatness, but he alone is the really great man whose character is great always, the same wherever he be.

Karma in its effect on character is the most tremendous power that man has to deal with. Man is, as it were, a centre, and is attracting all the powers of the universe towards himself, and in this centre is fusing them all and again sending them off in a big current. Such a centre is the *real* man — the almighty, the omniscient — and he draws the whole universe towards him. Good and bad, misery and happiness, all are running towards him and clinging round him; and out of them he fashions the mighty stream of tendency called character and throws it outwards. As he has the power of drawing in anything, so has he the power of throwing it out.

All the actions that we see in the world, all the movements in human society, all the works that we have around us, are simply the display of thought, the manifestation of the will of man. Machines or instruments, cities, ships, or men-of-war, all these are simply the manifestation of the will of man; and this will is caused by character, and character is manufactured by Karma. As is Karma, so is the manifestation of the will. The men of mighty will the world has produced have all been tremendous workers — gigantic souls, with wills powerful enough to overturn worlds, wills they got by persistent work, through ages, and ages. Such a gigantic will as that of a Buddha or a Jesus could not be obtained in one life, for we know who their fathers were. It is not known that their fathers ever spoke a word for the good of mankind. Millions and millions of carpenters like Joseph had gone; millions are still living. Millions and millions of petty kings like Buddha's father had been in the world. If it was only a case of hereditary transmission, how do you account for this petty prince, who was not, perhaps, obeyed by his own servants, producing this son, whom half a world worships? How do you explain the gulf between the carpenter and his son, whom millions of human beings worship as God? It cannot be solved by the theory of heredity. The gigantic will which Buddha and Jesus threw over the world, whence did it come? Whence came this accumulation of power? It must have been there through ages and ages, continually growing bigger and bigger, until it burst on society in a Buddha or a Jesus, even rolling down to the present day.

All this is determined by Karma, work. No one can get anything unless he earns it. This is an eternal law. We may sometimes think it is not so, but in the long run we become convinced of it. A man may struggle all his life for riches; he may cheat thousands, but he finds at last that he did not deserve to become rich, and his life becomes a trouble and a nuisance to him. We may go on accumulating things for our physical enjoyment, but only what we earn is really ours. A fool may buy all the books in the world, and they will be in his library; but he will be able to read only those that he deserves to; and this deserving is produced by Karma. Our Karma determines what we deserve and what we can assimilate. We are responsible for what we are; and whatever we wish ourselves to be, we have the power to make ourselves. If what we are now has been the result of our own past actions, it certainly follows that whatever we wish to be in future can be produced by our present actions; so we have to know how to act. You will say, "What is the use of learning how to work? Everyone works in some way or other in this world." But there is such a thing as frittering away our energies. With regard to Karma-Yoga, the Gita says that it is doing work with cleverness and as a science; by knowing how to work, one can obtain the greatest results. You must remember that all work is simply to bring out the power of the mind which is already there, to wake up the soul. The power is inside every man, so is knowing; the different works are like blows to bring them out, to cause these giants to wake up.

Man works with various motives. There cannot be work without motive. Some people want to get fame, and they work for fame. Others want money, and they work for money. Others want to have power, and they work for power. Others want to get to heaven, and they work for the same. Others want to leave a name when they die, as they do in China, where no man gets a title until he is dead; and that is a better way, after all, than with us. When a man does something very good there, they give a title of nobility to his father, who is dead, or to his grandfather. Some people work for that. Some of the followers of certain Mohammedan sects work all their lives to have a big tomb built for them when they die. I know sects among whom, as soon as a child is born, a tomb is prepared for it; that is among them the most important work a man has to do, and the bigger and the finer the tomb, the better off the man is supposed to be. Others work as a penance; do all sorts of wicked things, then erect a temple, or give something to the priests to buy them off and obtain from them a passport to heaven. They think that this kind of beneficence will clear them and they will go scot-free in spite of their sinfulness. Such are some of the various motives for work.

Work for work's sake. There are some who are really the salt of the earth in every country and who work for work's sake, who do not care for name, or fame, or even to go to heaven. They work just because good will come of it. There are others who do good to the poor and help mankind from still higher motives, because they believe in doing good and love good. The motive for name and fame seldom brings immediate results, as a rule; they come to us when we are old and have almost done with life. If a man works without any selfish motive in view, does he not gain anything? Yes, he gains the highest. Unselfishness is more paying, only people have not the patience to practice it. It is more paying from the point of view of health also. Love, truth, and unselfishness are not merely moral figures of speech, but they form our highest ideal, because in them lies such a manifestation of power. In the first place, a man who can work for five days, or even for five minutes, without any selfish motive whatever, without thinking of future, of heaven, of punishment, or anything of the kind, has in him the capacity to become a powerful moral giant. It is hard to do it, but in the heart of our hearts we know its value, and the good it brings. It is the greatest manifestation of power — this tremendous restraint; self-restraint is a manifestation of greater power than all outgoing action. A carriage with four horses may rush down a hill unrestrained, or the coachman may curb the horses. Which is the greater manifestation of power, to let them go or to hold them? A cannonball flying through the air goes a long distance and falls. Another is cut short in its flight by striking against a wall, and the impact generates intense heat. All outgoing energy following a selfish motive is frittered away; it will not cause power to return to you; but if restrained, it will result in development of power. This self-control will tend to produce a mighty will, a character which makes a Christ or a Buddha. Foolish men do not know this secret; they nevertheless want to rule mankind. Even a fool may rule the whole world if he works and waits. Let him wait a few years, restrain that foolish idea of governing; and when that idea is wholly gone, he will be a power in the world. The majority of us cannot see beyond a few years, just as some animals cannot see beyond a few steps. Just a little narrow circle — that is our world. We have not the patience to look beyond, and thus become immoral and wicked. This is our weakness, our powerlessness.

Even the lowest forms of work are not to be despised. Let the man, who knows no better, work for selfish ends, for name and fame; but everyone should always try to get towards higher and higher motives and to understand them. "To work we have the right, but not to the fruits thereof:" Leave the fruits alone. Why care for results? If you wish to help a man, never think what that man's attitude should be towards you. If you want to do a great or a good work, do not trouble to think what the result will be.

There arises a difficult question in this ideal of work. Intense activity is necessary; we must always work. We cannot live a minute without work. What then becomes of rest? Here is one side of the life-struggle — work, in which we are whirled rapidly round. And here is the other — that of calm, retiring renunciation: everything is peaceful around, there is very little of noise and show, only nature with her animals and flowers and mountains. Neither of them is a perfect picture. A man used to solitude, if brought in contact with the surging whirlpool of the world, will be crushed by it; just as the fish that lives in the deep sea water, as soon as it is brought to the surface, breaks into pieces, deprived of the weight of water on it that had kept it together. Can a man who has been used to the turmoil and the rush of life live at ease if he comes to a quiet place? He suffers and perchance may lose his mind. The ideal man is he who, in the midst of the greatest silence and solitude, finds the intensest activity, and in the midst of the intensest activity finds the silence and solitude of the desert. He has learnt the secret of restraint, he has controlled himself. He goes through the streets of a big city with all its traffic, and his mind is as calm as if he were in a cave, where not a sound could reach him; and he is intensely working all the time. That is the ideal of Karma-Yoga, and if you have attained to that you have really learnt the secret of work.

But we have to begin from the beginning, to take up the works as they come to us and slowly make ourselves more unselfish every day. We must do the work and find out the motive power that prompts us; and, almost without exception, in the first years, we shall find that our motives are always selfish; but gradually this selfishness will melt by persistence, till at last will come the time when we shall be able to do really unselfish work. We may all hope that some day or other, as we struggle through the paths of life, there will come a time when we shall become perfectly unselfish; and the moment we attain to that, all our powers will be concentrated, and the knowledge which is ours will be manifest.

CHAPTER II
Each is Great in His Own Place

According to the Sânkhya philosophy, nature is composed of three forces called, in Sanskrit, Sattva, Rajas, and Tamas. These as manifested in the physical world are what we may call equilibrium, activity, and inertness. Tamas is typified as darkness or inactivity; Rajas is activity, expressed as attraction or repulsion; and Sattva is the equilibrium of the two.

In every man there are these three forces. Sometimes Tamas prevails. We become lazy, we cannot move, we are inactive, bound down by certain ideas or by mere dullness. At other times activity prevails, and at still other times that calm balancing of both. Again, in different men, one of these forces is generally predominant. The characteristic of one man is inactivity, dullness and laziness; that of another, activity, power, manifestation of energy; and in still another we find the sweetness, calmness, and gentleness, which are due to the balancing of both action and inaction. So in all creation — in animals, plants, and men — we find the more or less typical manifestation of all these different forces.

Karma-Yoga has specially to deal with these three factors. By teaching what they are and how to employ them, it helps us to do our work better. Human society is a graded organization. We all know about morality, and we all know about duty, but at the same time we find that in different countries the significance of morality varies greatly. What is regarded as moral in one country may in another be considered perfectly immoral. For instance, in one country cousins may marry; in another, it is thought to be very immoral; in one, men may marry their sisters-in-law; in another, it is regarded as immoral; in one country people may marry only once; in another, many times; and so forth. Similarly, in all other departments of morality, we find the standard varies greatly — yet we have the idea that there must be a universal standard of morality.

So it is with duty. The idea of duty varies much among different nations. In one country, if a man does not do certain things, people will say he has acted wrongly; while if he does those very things in another country, people will say that he did not act rightly — and yet we know that there must be some universal idea of duty. In the same way, one class of society thinks that certain things are among its duty, while another class thinks quite the opposite and would be horrified if it had to do those things. Two ways are left open to us — the way of the ignorant, who think that there is only one way to truth and that all the rest are wrong, and the way of the wise, who admit that, according to our mental constitution or the different planes of existence in which we are, duty and morality may vary. The important thing is to know that there are gradations of duty and of morality — that the duty of one state of life, in one set of circumstances, will not and cannot be that of another.

To illustrate: All great teachers have taught, "Resist not evil," that non-resistance is the highest moral ideal. We all know that, if a certain number of us attempted to put that maxim fully into practice, the whole social fabric would fall to pieces, the wicked would take possession of our properties and our lives, and would do whatever they liked with us. Even if only one day of such non-resistance were practiced, it would lead to disaster. Yet, intuitively, in our heart of hearts we feel the truth of the teaching "Resist not evil." This seems to us to be the highest ideal; yet to teach this doctrine only would be equivalent to condemning a vast portion of mankind. Not only so, it would be making men feel that they were always doing wrong, and cause in them scruples of conscience in all their actions; it would weaken them, and that constant self-disapproval would breed more vice than any other weakness would. To the man who has begun to hate himself the gate to degeneration has already opened; and the same is true of a nation.

Our first duty is not to hate ourselves, because to advance we must have faith in ourselves first and then in God. He who has no faith in himself can never have faith in God. Therefore, the only alternative remaining to us is to recognise that duty and morality vary under different circumstances; not that the man who resists evil is doing what is always and in itself wrong, but that in the different circumstances in which he is placed it may become even his duty to resist evil.

In reading the Bhagavad-Gita, many of you in Western countries may have felt astonished at the second chapter, wherein Shri Krishna calls Arjuna a hypocrite and a coward because of his refusal to fight, or offer resistance, on account of his adversaries being his friends and relatives, making the plea that non-resistance was the highest ideal of love. This is a great lesson for us all to learn, that in all matters the two extremes are alike. The extreme positive and the extreme negative are always similar. When the vibrations of light are too slow, we do not see them, nor do we see them when they are too rapid. So with sound; when very low in pitch, we do not hear it; when very high, we do not hear it either. Of like nature is the difference between resistance and non-resistance. One man does not resist because he is weak, lazy, and cannot, not because he will not; the other man knows that he can strike an irresistible blow if he likes; yet he not only does not strike, but blesses his enemies. The one who from weakness resists not commits a sin, and as such cannot receive any benefit from the non-resistance; while theother would commit a sin by offering resistance. Buddha gave up his throne and renounced his position, that was true renunciation; but there cannot be any question of renunciation in the case of a beggar who has nothing to renounce. So we must always be careful about what we really mean when we speak of this non-resistance and ideal love. We must first take care to understand whether we have the power of resistance or not. Then, having the power, if we renounce it and do not resist, we are doing a grand act of love; but if we cannot resist, and yet, at the same time, try to deceive ourselves into the belief that we are actuated by motives of the highest love, we are doing the exact opposite. Arjuna became a coward at the sight of the mighty array against him; his "love" made him forget his duty towards his country and king. That is why Shri Krishna told him that he was a hypocrite: Thou talkest like a wise man, but thy actions betray thee to be a coward; therefore stand up and fight!

Such is the central idea of Karma-Yoga. The Karma-Yogi is the man who understands that the highest ideal is non-resistance, and who also knows that this non-resistance is the highest manifestation of power in actual possession, and also what is called the resisting of evil is but a step on the way towards the manifestation of this highest power, namely, non-resistance. Before reaching this highest ideal, man's duty is to resist evil; let him work, let him fight, let him strike straight from the shoulder.

Then only, when he has gained the power to resist, will non-resistance be a virtue.

I once met a man in my country whom I had known before as a very stupid, dull person, who knew nothing and had not the desire to know anything, and was living the life of a brute. He asked me what he should do to know God, how he was to get free. "Can you tell a lie?" I asked him. "No," he replied. "Then you must learn to do so. It is better to tell a lie than to be a brute, or a log of wood. You are inactive; you have not certainly reached the highest state, which is beyond all actions, calm and serene; you are too dull even to do something wicked." That was an extreme case, of course, and I was joking with him; but what I meant was that a man must be active in order to pass through activity to perfect calmness.

Inactivity should be avoided by all means. Activity always means resistance. Resist all evils, mental and physical; and when you have succeeded in resisting, then will calmness come. It is very easy to say, "Hate nobody, resist not evil," but we know what that kind of thing generally means in practice. When the eyes of society are turned towards us, we may make a show of non-resistance, but in our hearts it is canker all the time. We feel the utter want of the calm of non-resistance; we feel that it would be better for us to resist. If you desire wealth, and know at the same time that the whole world regards him who aims at wealth as a very wicked man, you, perhaps, will not dare to plunge into the struggle for wealth, yet your mind will be running day and night after money. This is hypocrisy and will serve no purpose. Plunge into the world, and then, after a time, when you have suffered and enjoyed all that is in it, will renunciation come; then will calmness come. So fulfil your desire for power and everything else, and after you have fulfilled the desire, will come the time when you will know that they are all very little things; but until you have fulfilled this desire, until you have passed through that activity, it is impossible for you to come to the state of calmness, serenity, and self-surrender. These ideas of serenity and renunciation have been preached for thousands of years; everybody has heard of them from childhood, and yet we see very few in the world who have really reached that stage. I do not know if I have seen twenty persons in my life who are really calm and non-resisting, and I have travelled over half the world.

Every man should take up his own ideal and endeavour to accomplish it. That is a surer way of progress than taking up other men's ideals, which he can never hope to accomplish. For instance, we take a child and at once give him the task of walking twenty miles. Either the little one dies, or one in a thousand crawls the twenty miles, to reach the end exhausted and half-dead. That is like what we generally try to do with the world. All the men and women, in any society, are not of the same mind, capacity, or of the same power to do things; they must have different ideals, and we have no right to sneer at any ideal. Let every one do the best he can for realising his own ideal. Nor is it right that I should be judged by your standard or you by mine. The apple tree should not be judged by the standard of the oak, nor the oak by that of the apple. To judge the apple tree you must take the apple standard, and for the oak, its own standard.

Unity in variety is the plan of creation. However men and women may vary individually, there is unity in the background. The different individual characters and classes of men and women are natural variations in creation. Hence, we ought not to judge them by the same standard or put the same ideal before them. Such a course creates only an unnatural struggle, and the result is that man begins to hate himself and is hindered from becoming religious and good. Our duty is to encourage every one in his struggle to live up to his own highest ideal, and strive at the same time to make the ideal as near as possible to the truth.

In the Hindu system of morality we find that this fact has been recognised from very ancient times; and in their scriptures and books on ethics different rules are laid down for the different classes of men — the householder, the Sannyâsin (the man who has renounced the world), and the student.

The life of every individual, according to the Hindu scriptures, has its peculiar duties apart from what belongs in common to universal humanity. The Hindu begins life as a student; then he marries and becomes a householder; in old age he retires; and lastly he gives up the world and becomes a Sannyasin. To each of these stages of life certain duties are attached. No one of these stages is intrinsically superior to another. The life of the married man is quite as great as that of the celibate who has devoted himself to religious work. The scavenger in the street is quite as great and glorious as the king on his throne. Take him off his throne, make him do the work of the scavenger, and see how he fares. Take up the scavenger and see how he will rule. It is useless to say that the man who lives out of the world is a greater man than he who lives in the world; it is much more difficult to live in the world and worship God than to give it up and live a free and easy life. The four stages of life in India have in later times been reduced to two — that of the householder and of the monk. The householder marries and carries on his duties as a citizen, and the duty of the other is to devote his energies wholly to religion, to preach and to worship God. I shall read to you a few passages from the Mahâ-Nirvâna-Tantra, which treats of this subject, and you will see that it is a very difficult task for a man to be a householder, and perform all his duties perfectly:

The householder should be devoted to God; the knowledge of God should be his goal of life. Yet he must work constantly, perform all his duties; he must give up the fruits of his actions to God.

It is the most difficult thing in this world to work and not care for the result, to help a man and never think that he ought to be grateful, to do some good work and at the same time never look to see whether it brings you name or fame, or nothing at all. Even the most arrant coward becomes brave when the world praises him. A fool can do heroic deeds when the approbation of society is upon him, but for a man to constantly do good without caring for the approbation of his fellow men is indeed the highest sacrifice man can perform. The great duty of the householder is to earn a living, but he must take care that he does not do it by telling lies, or by cheating, or by robbing others; and he must remember that his life is for the service of God, and the poor.

Knowing that mother and father are the visible representatives of God, the householder, always and by all means, must please them. If the mother is pleased, and the father, God is pleased with the man. That child is really a good child who never speaks harsh words to his parents.

Before parents one must not utter jokes, must not show restlessness, must not show anger or temper. Before mother or father, a child must bow down low, and stand up in their presence, and must not take a seat until they order him to sit.

If the householder has food and drink and clothes without first seeing that his mother and his father, his children, his wife, and the poor, are supplied, he is committing a sin. The mother and the father are the causes of this body; so a man must undergo a thousand troubles in order to do good to them.

Even so is his duty to his wife. No man should scold his wife, and he must always maintain her as if she were his own mother. And even when he is in the greatest difficulties and troubles, he must not show anger to his wife.

He who thinks of another woman besides his wife, if he touches her even with his mind — that man goes to dark hell.

Before women he must not talk improper language, and never brag of his powers. He must not say, "I have done this, and I have done that."

The householder must always please his wife with money, clothes, love, faith, and words like nectar, and never do anything to disturb her. That man who has succeeded in getting the love of a chaste wife has succeeded in his religion and has all the virtues.

The following are duties towards children:

A son should be lovingly reared up to his fourth year; he should be educated till he is sixteen. When he is twenty years of age he should be employed in some work; he should then be treated affectionately by his father as his equal. Exactly in the same manner the daughter should be brought up, and should be educated with the greatest care. And when she marries, the father ought to give her jewels and wealth.

Then the duty of the man is towards his brothers and sisters, and towards the children of his brothers and sisters, if they are poor, and towards his other relatives, his friends and his servants. Then his duties are towards the people of the same village, and the poor, and any one that comes to him for help. Having sufficient means, if the householder does not take care to give to his relatives and to the poor, know him to be only a brute; he is not a human being.

Excessive attachment to food, clothes, and the tending of the body, and dressing of the hair should be avoided. The householder must be pure in heart and clean in body, always active and always ready for work.

To his enemies the householder must be a hero. Them he must resist. That is the duty of the householder. He must not sit down in a corner and weep, and talk nonsense about non-resistance. If he does not show himself a hero to his enemies he has not done his duty. And to his friends and relatives he must be as gentle as a lamb.

It is the duty of the householder not to pay reverence to the wicked; because, if he reverences the wicked people of the world, he patronizes wickedness; and it will be a great mistake if he disregards those who are worthy of respect, the good people. He must not be gushing in his friendship; he must not go out of the way making friends everywhere; he must watch the actions of the men he wants to make friends with, and their dealings with other men, reason upon them, and then make friends.

These three things he must not talk of. He must not talk in public of his own fame; he must not preach his own name or his own powers; he must not talk of his wealth, or of anything that has been told to him privately.

A man must not say he is poor, or that he is wealthy — he must not brag of his wealth. Let him keep his own counsel; this is his religious duty. This is not mere worldly wisdom; if a man does not do so, he may be held to be immoral.

The householder is the basis, the prop, of the whole society. He is the principal earner. The poor, the weak, the children and the women who do not work — all live upon the householder; so there must be certain duties that he has to perform, and these duties must make him feel strong to perform them, and not make him think that he is doing things beneath his ideal. Therefore, if he has done something weak, or has made some mistake, he must not say so in public; and if he is engaged in some enterprise and knows he is sure to fail in it, he must not speak of it. Such self-exposure is not only uncalled for, but also unnerves the man and makes him unfit for the performance of his legitimate duties in life. At the same time, he must struggle hard to acquire these things — firstly, knowledge, and secondly, wealth. It is his duty, and if he does not do his duty, he is nobody. A householder who does not struggle to get wealth is immoral. If he is lazy and content to lead an idle life, he is immoral, because upon him depend hundreds. If he gets riches, hundreds of others will be thereby supported.

If there were not in this city hundreds who had striven to become rich, and who had acquired wealth, where would all this civilization, and these alms-houses and great houses be?

Going after wealth in such a case is not bad, because that wealth is for distribution. The householder is the centre of life and society. It is a worship for him to acquire and spend wealth nobly, for the householder who struggles to become rich by good means and for good purposes is doing practically the same thing for the attainment of salvation as the anchorite does in his cell when he is praying; for in them we see only the different aspects of the same virtue of self-surrender and self-sacrifice prompted by the feeling of devotion to God and to all that is His.

He must struggle to acquire a good name by all means. He must not gamble, he must not move in the company of the wicked, he must not tell lies, and must not be the cause of trouble to others.

Often people enter into things they have not the means to accomplish, with the result that they cheat others to attain their own ends. Then there is in all things the time factor to be taken into consideration; what at one time might be a failure, would perhaps at another time be a very great success.

The householder must speak the truth, and speak gently, using words which people like, which will do good to others; nor should he talk of the business of other men.

The householder by digging tanks, by planting trees on the roadsides, by establishing rest-houses for men and animals, by making roads and building bridges, goes towards the same goal as the greatest Yogi.

This is one part of the doctrine of Karma-Yoga — activity, the duty of the householder. There is a passage later on, where it says that "if the householder dies in battle, fighting for his country or his religion, he comes to the same goal as the Yogi by meditation," showing thereby that what is duty for one is not duty for another. At the same time, it does not say that this duty is lowering and the other elevating. Each duty has its own place, and according to the circumstances in which we are placed, we must perform our duties.

One idea comes out of all this — the condemnation of all weakness. This is a particular idea in all our teachings which I like, either in philosophy, or in religion, or in work. If you read the Vedas, you will find this word always repeated — fearlessness — fear nothing. Fear is a sign of weakness. A man must go about his duties without taking notice of the sneers and the ridicule of the world.

If a man retires from the world to worship God, he must not think that those who live in the world and work for the good of the world are not worshipping God: neither must those who live in the world, for wife and children, think that those who give up the world are low vagabonds. Each is great in his own place. This thought I will illustrate by a story.

A certain king used to inquire of all the Sannyasins that came to his country, "Which is the greater man — he who gives up the world and becomes a Sannyasin, or he who lives in the world and performs his duties as a house holder?" Many wise men sought to solve the problem. Some asserted that the Sannyasin was the greater, upon which the king demanded that they should prove their assertion. When they could not, he ordered them to marry and become householders. Then others came and said, "The householder who performs his duties is the greater man." Of them, too, the king demanded proofs. When they could not give them, he made them also settle down as householders.

At last there came a young Sannyasin, and the king similarly inquired of him also. He answered, "Each, O king, is equally great in his place." "Prove this to me," asked the king. "I will prove it to you," said the Sannyasin, "but you must first come and live as I do for a few days, that I may be able to prove to you what I say." The king consented and followed the Sannyasin out of his own territory and passed through many other countries until they came to a great kingdom. In the capital of that kingdom a great ceremony was going on. The king and the Sannyasin heard the noise of drums and music, and heard also the criers; the people were assembled in the streets in gala dress, and a great proclamation was being made. The king and the Sannyasin stood there to see what was going on. The crier was proclaiming loudly that the princess, daughter of the king of that country, was about to choose a husband from among those assembled before her.

It was an old custom in India for princesses to choose husbands in this way. Each princess had certain ideas of the sort of man she wanted for a husband. Some would have the handsomest man, others would have only the most learned, others again the richest, and so on. All the princes of the neighbourhood put on their bravest attire and presented themselves before her. Sometimes they too had their own criers to enumerate their advantages and the reasons why they hoped the princess would choose them. The princess was taken round on a throne, in the most splendid array, and looked at and heard about them. If she was not pleased with what she saw and heard, she said to her bearers, "Move on," and no more notice was taken of the rejected suitors. If, however, the princess was pleased with any one of them, she threw a garland of flowers over him and he became her husband.

The princess of the country to which our king and the Sannyasin had come was having one of these interesting ceremonies. She was the most beautiful princess in the world, and the husband of the princess would be ruler of the kingdom after her father's death. The idea of this princess was to marry the handsomest man, but she could not find the right one to please her. Several times these meetings had taken place, but the princess could not select a husband. This meeting was the most splendid of all;

more people than ever had come to it. The princess came in on a throne, and the bearers carried her from place to place. She did not seem to care for any one, and every one became disappointed that this meeting also was going to be a failure. Just then came a young man, a Sannyasin, handsome as if the sun had come down to the earth, and stood in one corner of the assembly, watching what was going on. The throne with the princess came near him, and as soon as she saw the beautiful Sannyasin, she stopped and threw the garland over him. The young Sannyasin seized the garland and threw it off, exclaiming, "What nonsense is this? I am a Sannyasin. What is marriage to me?" The king of that country thought that perhaps this man was poor and so dared not marry the princess, and said to him, "With my daughter goes half my kingdom now, and the whole kingdom after my death!" and put the garland again on the Sannyasin. The young man threw it off once more, saying, "Nonsense! I do not want to marry," and walked quickly away from the assembly.

Now the princess had fallen so much in love with this young man that she said, "I must marry this man or I shall die"; and she went after him to bring him back. Then our other Sannyasin, who had brought the king there, said to him, "King, let us follow this pair"; so they walked after them, but at a good distance behind. The young Sannyasin who had refused to marry the princess walked out into the country for several miles. When he came to a forest and entered into it, the princess followed him, and the other two followed them. Now this young Sannyasin was well acquainted with that forest and knew all the intricate paths in it. He suddenly passed into one of these and disappeared, and the princess could not discover him. After trying for a long time to find him she sat down under a tree and began to weep, for she did not know the way out. Then our king and the other Sannyasin came up to her and said, "Do not weep; we will show you the way out of this forest, but it is too dark for us to find it now. Here is a big tree; let us rest under it, and in the morning we will go early and show you the road."

Now a little bird and his wife and their three little ones lived on that tree, in a nest. This little bird looked down and saw the three people under the tree and said to his wife, "My dear, what shall we do? Here are some guests in the house, and it is winter, and we have no fire." So he flew away and got a bit of burning firewood in his beak and dropped it before the guests, to which they added fuel and made a blazing fire. But the little bird was not satisfied. He said again to his wife, "My dear, what shall we do? There is nothing to give these people to eat, and they are hungry. We are householders; it is our duty to feed any one who comes to the house. I must do what I can, I will give them my body." So he plunged into the midst of the fire and perished. The guests saw him falling and tried to save him, but he was too quick for them.

The little bird's wife saw what her husband did, and she said, "Here are three persons and only one little bird for them to eat. It is not enough; it is my duty as a wife not to let my husband's effort go in vain; let them have my body also." Then she fell into the fire and was burned to death.

Then the three baby-birds, when they saw what was done and that there was still not enough food for the three guests, said, "Our parents have done what they could and still it is not enough. It is our duty to carry on the work of our parents; let our bodies go too." And they all dashed down into the fire also.

Amazed at what they saw, the three people could not of course eat these birds. They passed the night without food, and in the morning the king and the Sannyasin showed the princess the way, and she went back to her father.

Then the Sannyasin said to the king, "King, you have seen that each is great in his own place. If you want to live in the world, live like those birds, ready at any moment to sacrifice yourself for others. If you want to renounce the world, be like that young man to whom the most beautiful woman and a kingdom were as nothing. If you want to be a householder, hold your life a sacrifice for the welfare of others; and if you choose the life of renunciation, do not even look at beauty and money and power. Each is great in his own place, but the duty of the one is not the duty of the other.

CHAPTER III
The Secret of Work

Helping others physically, by removing their physical needs, is indeed great, but the help is great according as the need is greater and according as the help is far reaching. If a man's wants can be removed for an hour, it is helping him indeed; if his wants can be removed for a year, it will be more help to him; but if his wants can be removed for ever, it is surely the greatest help that can be given him. Spiritual knowledge is the only thing that can destroy our miseries for ever; any other knowledge satisfies wants only for a time. It is only with the knowledge of the spirit that the faculty of want is annihilated for ever; so helping man spiritually is the highest help that can be given to him. He who gives man spiritual knowledge is the greatest benefactor of mankind and as such we always find that those were the most powerful of men who helped man in his spiritual needs, because spirituality is the true basis of all our activities in life. A spiritually strong and sound man will be strong in every other respect, if he so wishes. Until there is spiritual strength in man even physical needs cannot be well satisfied. Next to spiritual comes intellectual help. The gift of knowledge is a far higher gift than that of food and clothes; it is even higher than giving life to a man, because the real life of man consists of knowledge. Ignorance is death, knowledge is life. Life is of very little value, if it is a life in the dark, groping through ignorance and misery. Next in order comes, of course, helping a man physically. Therefore, in considering the question of helping others, we must always strive not to commit the mistake of thinking that physical help is the only help that can be given. It is not only the last but the least, because it cannot bring about permanent satisfaction. The misery that I feel when I am hungry is satisfied by eating, but hunger returns; my misery can cease only when I am satisfied beyond all want. Then hunger will not make me miserable; no distress, no sorrow will be able to move me. So, that help which tends to make us strong spiritually is the highest, next to it comes intellectual help, and after that physical help.

The miseries of the world cannot be cured by physical help only. Until man's nature changes, these physical needs will always arise, and miseries will always be felt, and no amount of physical help will cure them completely. The only solution of this problem is to make mankind pure. Ignorance is the mother of all the evil and all the misery we see. Let men have light, let them be pure and spiritually strong and educated, then alone will misery cease in the world, not before. We may convert every house in the country into a charity asylum, we may fill the land with hospitals, but the misery of man will still continue to exist until man's character changes.

We read in the Bhagavad-Gita again and again that we must all work incessantly. All work is by nature composed of good and evil. We cannot do any work which will not do some good somewhere; there cannot be any work which will not cause some harm somewhere. Every work must necessarily be a mixture of good and evil; yet we are commanded to work incessantly. Good and evil will both have their results, will produce their Karma. Good action will entail upon us good effect; bad action, bad. But good and bad are both bondages of the soul. The solution reached in the Gita in regard to this bondage-producing nature of work is that, if we do not attach ourselves to the work we do, it will not have any binding effect on our soul. We shall try to understand what is meant by this "non-attachment to" to work.

This is the one central idea in the Gita: work incessantly, but be not attached to it. Samskâra can be translated very nearly by "inherent tendency". Using the simile of a lake for the mind, every ripple, every wave that rises in the mind, when it subsides, does not die out entirely, but leaves a mark and a future possibility of that wave coming out again. This mark, with the possibility of the wave reappearing, is what is called Samskâra. Every work that we do, every movement of the body, every thought that we think, leaves such an impression on the mind-stuff, and even when such impressions are not obvious on the surface, they are sufficiently strong to work beneath the surface, subconsciously. What we are every moment is determined by the sum total of these impressions on the mind. What I am just at this moment is the effect of the sum total of all the impressions of my past life. This is really what is meant by character; each man's character is determined by the sum total of these impressions. If good impressions prevail, the character becomes good; if bad, it becomes bad. If a man continuously hears bad words, thinks bad thoughts, does bad actions, his mind will be full of bad impressions; and they will influence his thought and work without his being conscious of the fact. In fact, these bad impressions are always working, and their resultant must be evil, and that man will be a bad man; he cannot help it. The sum total of these impressions in him will create the strong motive power for doing bad actions. He will be like a machine in the hands of his impressions, and they will force him to do evil. Similarly, if a man thinks good thoughts and does good works, the sum total of these impressions will be good; and they, in a similar manner, will force him to do good even in spite of himself. When a man has done so much good work and thought so many good thoughts that there is an irresistible tendency in him to do good in spite of himself and even if he wishes to do evil, his mind, as the sum total of his tendencies, will not allow him to do so; the tendencies will turn him back; he is completely under the influence of the good tendencies. When such is the case, a man's good character is said to be established.

As the tortoise tucks its feet and head inside the shell, and you may kill it and break it in pieces, and yet it will not come out, even so the character of that man who has control over his motives and organs is unchangeably established. He controls his own inner forces, and nothing can draw them out against his will. By this continuous reflex of good thoughts, good impressions moving over the surface of the mind, the tendency for doing good becomes strong, and as the result we feel able to control the Indriyas (the sense-organs, the nerve-centres). Thus alone will character be established, then alone a man gets to truth. Such a man is safe for ever; he cannot do any evil. You may place him in any company, there will be no danger for him. There is a still higher state than having this good tendency, and that is the desire for liberation. You must remember that freedom of the soul is the goal of all Yogas, and each one equally leads to the same result. By work alone men may get to where Buddha got largely by meditation or Christ by prayer. Buddha was a working Jnâni, Christ was a Bhakta, but the same goal was reached by both of them. The difficulty is here. Liberation means entire freedom — freedom from the bondage of good, as well as from the bondage of evil. A golden chain is as much a chain as an iron one. There is a thorn in my finger, and I use another to take the first one out; and when I have taken it out, I throw both of them aside; I have no necessity for keeping the second thorn, because both are thorns after all. So the bad tendencies are to be counteracted by the good ones, and the bad impressions on the mind should be removed by the fresh waves of good ones, until all that is evil almost disappears, or is subdued and held in control in a corner of the mind; but after that, the good tendencies have also to be conquered. Thus the "attached" becomes the "unattached". Work, but let not the action or the thought produce a deep impression on the mind. Let the ripples come and go, let huge actions proceed from the muscles and the brain, but let them not make any deep impression on the soul.

How can this be done? We see that the impression of any action, to which we attach ourselves, remains. I may meet hundreds of persons during the day, and among them meet also one whom I love; and when I retire at night, I may try to think of all the faces I saw, but only that face comes before the mind — the face which I met perhaps only for one minute, and which I loved; all the others have vanished. My attachment to this particular person caused a deeper impression on my mind than all the other faces. Physiologically the impressions have all been the same; every one of the faces that I saw pictured itself on the retina, and the brain took the pictures in, and yet there was no similarity of effect upon the mind. Most of the faces, perhaps, were entirely new faces, about which I had never thought before, but that one face of which I got only a glimpse found associations inside. Perhaps I had pictured him in my mind for years, knew hundreds of things about him, and this one new vision of him awakened hundreds of sleeping memories in my mind; and this one impression having been repeated perhaps a hundred times more than those of the different faces together, will produce a great effect on the mind.

Therefore, be "unattached"; let things work; let brain centres work; work incessantly, but let not a ripple conquer the mind. Work as if you were a stranger in this land, a sojourner; work incessantly, but do not bind yourselves; bondage is terrible. This world is not our habitation, it is only one of the many stages through which we are passing. Remember that great saying of the Sânkhya, "The whole of nature is for the soul, not the soul for nature." The very reason of nature's existence is for the education of the soul; it has no other meaning; it is there because the soul must have knowledge, and through knowledge free itself. If we remember this always, we shall never be attached to nature; we shall know that nature is a book in which we are to read, and that when we have gained the required knowledge, the book is of no more value to us. Instead of that, however, we are identifying ourselves with nature; we are thinking that the soul is for nature, that the spirit is for the flesh, and, as the common saying has it, we think that man "lives to eat" and not "eats to live". We are continually making this mistake; we are regarding nature as ourselves and are becoming attached to it; and as soon as this attachment comes, there is the deep impression on the soul, which binds us down and makes us work not from freedom but like slaves.

The whole gist of this teaching is that you should work like a *master* and not as a *slave*; work incessantly, but do not do slave's work. Do you not see how everybody works? Nobody can be altogether at rest; ninety-nine per cent of mankind work like slaves, and the result is misery; it is all selfish work. Work through freedom! Work through love! The word "love" is very difficult to understand; love never comes until there is freedom. There is no true love possible in the slave. If you buy a slave and tie him down in chains and make him work for you, he will work like a drudge, but there will be no love in him. So when we ourselves work for the things of the world as slaves, there can be no love in us, and our work is not true work. This is true of work done for relatives and friends, and is true of work done for our own selves. Selfish work is slave's work; and here is a test. Every act of love brings happiness; there is no act of love which does not bring peace and blessedness as its reaction. Real existence, real knowledge, and real love are eternally connected with one another, the three in one: where one of them is, the others also must be; they are the three aspects of the One without a second — the Existence - Knowledge - Bliss. When that existence becomes relative, we see it as the world; that knowledge becomes in its turn modified into the knowledge of the things of the world; and that bliss forms the foundation of all true love known to the heart of man. Therefore true love can never react so as to cause pain either to the lover or to the beloved. Suppose a man loves a woman; he wishes to have her all to himself and feels extremely jealous about her every movement; he wants her to sit near him, to stand near him, and to eat and move at his bidding. He is a slave to her and wishes to have her as his slave. That is not love; it is a kind of morbid affection of the slave, insinuating itself as love. It cannot be love, because it is painful; if she does not do what he wants, it brings him pain. With love there is no painful reaction; love only brings a reaction of bliss; if it does not, it is not love; it is mistaking something else for love. When you have succeeded in loving your husband, your wife, your children, the whole world, the universe, in such a manner that there is no reaction of pain or jealousy, no selfish feeling, then you are in a fit state to be unattached.

Krishna says, "Look at Me, Arjuna! If I stop from work for one moment, the whole universe will die. I have nothing to gain from work; I am the one Lord, but why do I work? Because I love the world." God is unattached because He loves; that real love makes us unattached. Wherever there is attachment, the clinging to the things of the world, you must know that it is all physical attraction between sets of particles of matter — something that attracts two bodies nearer and nearer all the time and, if they cannot get near enough, produces pain; but where there is *real* love, it does not rest on physical attachment at all. Such lovers may be a thousand miles away from one another, but their love will be all the same; it does not die, and will never produce any painful reaction.

To attain this unattachment is almost a life-work, but as soon as we have reached this point, we have attained the goal of love and become free; the bondage of nature falls from us, and we see nature as she is; she forges no more chains for us; we stand entirely free and take not the results of work into consideration; who then cares for what the results may be?

Do you ask anything from your children in return for what you have given them? It is your duty to work for them, and there the matter ends. In whatever you do for a particular person, a city, or a state, assume the same attitude towards it as you have towards your children — expect nothing in return. If you can invariably take the position of a giver, in which everything given by you is a free offering to the world, without any thought of return, then will your work bring you no attachment. Attachment comes only where we expect a return.

If working like slaves results in selfishness and attachment, working as master of our own mind gives rise to the bliss of non-attachment. We often talk of right and justice, but we find that in the world right and justice are mere baby's talk. There are two things which guide the conduct of men: might and mercy. The exercise of might is invariably the exercise of selfishness. All men and women try to make the most of whatever power or advantage they have. Mercy is heaven itself; to be good, we have all to be merciful. Even justice and right should stand on mercy. All thought of obtaining return for the work we do hinders our spiritual progress; nay, in the end it brings misery. There is another way in which this idea of mercy and selfless charity can be put into practice; that is, by looking upon work as "worship" in case we believe in a Personal God. Here we give up all the fruits our work unto the Lord, and worshipping Him thus, we have no right to expect anything from mankind for the work we do. The Lord Himself works incessantly and is ever without attachment. Just as water cannot wet the lotus leaf, so work cannot bind the unselfish man by giving rise to attachment to results. The selfless and unattached man may live in the very heart of a crowded and sinful city; he will not be touched by sin.

This idea of complete self-sacrifice is illustrated in the following story: After the battle of Kurukshetra the five Pândava brothers performed a great sacrifice and made very large gifts to the poor. All people expressed amazement at the greatness and richness of the sacrifice, and said that such a sacrifice the world had never seen before. But, after the ceremony, there came a little mongoose, half of whose body was golden, and the other half brown; and he began to roll on the floor of the sacrificial hall. He said to those around, "You are all liars; this is no sacrifice." "What!" they exclaimed, "you say this is no sacrifice; do you not know how money and jewels were poured out to the poor and every one became rich and happy? This was the most wonderful sacrifice any man ever performed." But the mongoose said, "There was once a little village, and in it there dwelt a poor Brahmin with his wife, his son, and his son's wife. They were very poor and lived on small gifts made to them for preaching and teaching. There came in that land a three years' famine, and the poor Brahmin suffered more than ever. At last when the family had starved for days, the father brought home one morning a little barley flour, which he had been fortunate enough to obtain, and he divided it into four parts, one for each member of the family. They prepared it for their meal, and just as they were about to eat, there was a knock at the door. The father opened it, and there stood a guest. Now in India a guest is a sacred person; he is as a god for the time being, and must be treated as such. So the poor Brahmin said, 'Come in, sir; you are welcome,' He set before the guest his own portion of the food, which the guest quickly ate and said, 'Oh, sir, you have killed me; I have been starving for ten days, and this little bit has but increased my hunger.' Then the wife said to her husband, 'Give him my share,' but the husband said, 'Not so.' The wife however insisted, saying, 'Here is a poor man, and it is our duty as householders to see that he is fed, and it is my duty as a wife to give him my portion, seeing that you have no more to offer him.' Then she gave her share to the guest, which he ate, and said he was still burning with hunger. So the son said, 'Take my portion also; it is the duty of a son to help his father to fulfil his obligations.'

The guest ate that, but remained still unsatisfied; so the son's wife gave him her portion also. That was sufficient, and the guest departed, blessing them. That night those four people died of starvation. A few granules of that flour had fallen on the floor; and when I rolled my body on them, half of it became golden, as you see. Since then I have been travelling all over the world, hoping to find another sacrifice like that, but nowhere have I found one; nowhere else has the other half of my body been turned into gold. That is why I say this is no sacrifice."

This idea of charity is going out of India; great men are becoming fewer and fewer. When I was first learning English, I read an English story book in which there was a story about a dutiful boy who had gone out to work and had given some of his money to his old mother, and this was praised in three or four pages. What was that? No Hindu boy can ever understand the moral of that story. Now I understand it when I hear the Western idea — every man for himself. And some men take everything for themselves, and fathers and mothers and wives and children go to the wall. That should never and nowhere be the ideal of the householder.

Now you see what Karma-Yoga means; even at the point of death to help any one, without asking questions. Be cheated millions of times and never ask a question, and never think of what you are doing. Never vaunt of your gifts to the poor or expect their gratitude, but rather be grateful to them for giving you the occasion of practicing charity to them. Thus it is plain that to be an ideal householder is a much more difficult task than to be an ideal Sannyasin; the true life of work is indeed as hard as, if not harder than, the equally true life of renunciation.

CHAPTER IV
What is Duty?

It is necessary in the study of Karma-Yoga to know what duty is. If I have to do something I must first know that it is my duty, and then I can do it. The idea of duty again is different in different nations. The Mohammedan says what is written in his book, the Koran, is his duty; the Hindu says what is in the Vedas is his duty; and the Christian says what is in the Bible is his duty. We find that there are varied ideas of duty, differing according to different states in life, different historical periods and different nations. The term "duty", like every other universal abstract term, is impossible clearly to define; we can only get an idea of it by knowing its practical operations and results. When certain things occur before us, we have all a natural or trained impulse to act in a certain manner towards them; when this impulse comes, the mind begins to think about the situation. Sometimes it thinks that it is good to act in a particular manner under the given conditions; at other times it thinks that it is wrong to act in the same manner even in the very same circumstances. The ordinary idea of duty everywhere is that every good man follows the dictates of his conscience. But what is it that makes an act a duty? If a Christian finds a piece of beef before him and does not eat it to save his own life, or will not give it to save the life of another man, he is sure to feel that he has not done his duty. But if a Hindu dares to eat that piece of beef or to give it to another Hindu, he is equally sure to feel that he too has not done his duty; the Hindu's training and education make him feel that way. In the last century there were notorious bands of robbers in India called thugs; they thought it their duty to kill any man they could and take away his money; the larger the number of men they killed, the better they thought they were. Ordinarily if a man goes out into the street and shoots down another man, he is apt to feel sorry for it, thinking that he has done wrong. But if the very same man, as a soldier in his regiment, kills not one but twenty, he is certain to feel glad and think that he has done his duty remarkably well. Therefore we see that it is not the thing done that defines a duty. To give an objective definition of duty is thus entirely impossible. Yet there is duty from the subjective side. Any action that makes us go Godward is a good action, and is our duty; any action that makes us go downward is evil, and is not our duty. From the subjective standpoint we may see that certain acts have a tendency to exalt and ennoble us, while certain other acts have a tendency to degrade and to brutalise us. But it is not possible to make out with certainty which acts have which kind of tendency in relation to all persons, of all sorts and conditions. There is, however, only one idea of duty which has been universally accepted by all mankind, of all ages and sects and countries, and that has been summed up in a Sanskrit aphorism thus: "Do not injure any being; not injuring any being is virtue, injuring any being is sin."

The Bhagavad-Gita frequently alludes to duties dependent upon birth and position in life. Birth and position in life and in society largely determine the mental and moral attitude of individuals towards the various activities of life. It is therefore our duty to do that work which will exalt and ennoble us in accordance with the ideals and activities of the society in which we are born. But it must be particularly remembered that the same ideals and activities do not prevail in all societies and countries; our ignorance of this is the main cause of much of the hatred of one nation towards another. An American thinks that whatever an American does in accordance with the custom of his country is the best thing to do, and that whoever does not follow his custom must be a very wicked man. A Hindu thinks that his customs are the only right ones and are the best in the world, and that whosoever does not obey them must be the most wicked man living. This is quite a natural mistake which all of us are apt to make. But it is very harmful; it is the cause of half the uncharitableness found in the world. When I came to this country and was going through the Chicago Fair, a man from behind pulled at my turban. I looked back and saw that he was a very gentlemanly-looking man, neatly dressed. I spoke to him; and when he found that I knew English, he became very much abashed. On another occasion in the same Fair another man gave me a push. When I asked him the reason, he also was ashamed and stammered out an apology saying, "Why do you dress that way?" The sympathies of these men were limited within the range of their own language and their own fashion of dress. Much of the oppression of powerful nations on weaker ones is caused by this prejudice. It dries up their fellow feeling for fellow men. That very man who asked me why I did not dress as he did and wanted to ill-treat me because of my dress may have been a very good man, a good father, and a good citizen; but the kindliness of his nature died out as soon as he saw a man in a different dress. Strangers are exploited in all countries, because they do not know how to defend themselves; thus they carry home false impressions of the peoples they have seen. Sailors, soldiers, and traders behave in foreign lands in very queer ways, although they would not dream of doing so in their own country; perhaps this is why the Chinese call Europeans and Americans "foreign devils". They could not have done this if they had met the good, the kindly sides of Western life.

Therefore the one point we ought to remember is that we should always try to see the duty of others through their own eyes, and never judge the customs of other peoples by our own standard. I am not the standard of the universe. I have to accommodate myself to the world, and not the world to me. So we see that environments change the nature of our duties, and doing the duty which is ours at any particular time is the best thing we can do in this world. Let us do that duty which is ours by birth; and when we have done that, let us do the duty which is ours by our position in life and in society. There is, however, one great danger in human nature, viz that man never examines himself. He thinks he is quite as fit to be on the throne as the king. Even if he is, he must first show that he has done the duty of his own position; and then higher duties will come to him. When we begin to work earnestly in the world, nature gives us blows right and left and soon enables us to find out our position. No man can long occupy satisfactorily a position for which he is not fit. There is no use in grumbling against nature's adjustment. He who does the lower work is not therefore a lower man. No man is to be judged by the mere nature of his duties, but all should be judged by the manner and the spirit in which they perform them.

Later on we shall find that even this idea of duty undergoes change, and that the greatest work is done only when there is no selfish motive to prompt it. Yet it is work through the sense of duty that leads us to work without any idea of duty; when work will become worship — nay, something higher — then will work be done for its own sake. We shall find that the philosophy of duty, whether it be in the form of ethics or of love, is the same as in every other Yoga — the object being the attenuating of the lower self, so that the real higher Self may shine forth — the lessening of the frittering away of energies on the lower plane of existence, so that the soul may manifest itself on the higher ones. This is accomplished by the continuous denial of low desires, which duty rigorously requires. The whole organisation of society has thus been developed, consciously or unconsciously, in the realms of action and experience, where, by limiting selfishness, we open the way to an unlimited expansion of the real nature of man.

Duty is seldom sweet. It is only when love greases its wheels that it runs smoothly; it is a continuous friction otherwise. How else could parents do their duties to their children, husbands to their wives, and vice versa? Do we not meet with cases of friction every day in our lives? Duty is sweet only through love, and love shines in freedom alone. Yet is it freedom to be a slave to the senses, to anger, to jealousies and a hundred other petty things that must occur every day in human life? In all these little roughnesses that we meet with in life, the highest expression of freedom is to forbear. Women, slaves to their own irritable, jealous tempers, are apt to blame their husbands, and assert their own "freedom", as they think, not knowing that thereby they only prove that they are slaves. So it is with husbands who eternally find fault with their wives.

Chastity is the first virtue in man or woman, and the man who, however he may have strayed away, cannot be brought to the right path by a gentle and loving and chaste wife is indeed very rare. The world is not yet as bad as that. We hear much about brutal husbands all over the world and about the impurity of men, but is it not true that there are quite as many brutal and impure women as men? If all women were as good and pure as their own constant assertions would lead one to believe, I am perfectly satisfied that there would not be one impure man in the world. What brutality is there which purity and chastity cannot conquer? A good, chaste wife, who thinks of every other man except her own husband as her child and has the attitude of a mother towards all men, will grow so great in the power of her purity that there cannot be a single man, however brutal, who will not breathe an atmosphere of holiness in her presence. Similarly, every husband must look upon all women, except his own wife, in the light of his own mother or daughter or sister. That man, again, who wants to be a teacher of religion must look upon every woman as his mother, and always behave towards her as such.

The position of the mother is the highest in the world, as it is the one place in which to learn and exercise the greatest unselfishness. The love of God is the only love that is higher than a mother's love; all others are lower. It is the duty of the mother to think of her children first and then of herself. But, instead of that, if the parents are always thinking of themselves first, the result is that the relation between parents and children becomes the same as that between birds and their offspring which, as soon as they are fledged, do not recognise any parents. Blessed, indeed, is the man who is able to look upon woman as the representative of the motherhood of God. Blessed, indeed, is the woman to whom man represents the fatherhood of God. Blessed are the children who look upon their parents as Divinity manifested on earth.

The only way to rise is by doing the duty next to us, and thus gathering strength go on until we reach the highest state. A young Sannyâsin went to a forest; there he meditated, worshipped, and practiced Yoga for a long time. After years of hard work and practice, he was one day sitting under a tree, when some dry leaves fell upon his head. He looked up and saw a crow and a crane fighting on the top of the tree, which made him very angry. He said, "What! Dare you throw these dry leaves upon my head!" As with these words he angrily glanced at them, a flash of fire went out of his head — such was the Yogi's power — and burnt the birds to ashes. He was very glad, almost overjoyed at this development of power — he could burn the crow and the crane by a look. After a time he had to go to the town to beg his bread. He went, stood at a door, and said, "Mother, give me food." A voice came from inside the house, "Wait a little, my son." The young man thought, "You wretched woman, how dare you make me wait! You do not know my power yet." While he was thinking thus the voice came again: "Boy, don't be thinking too much of yourself. Here is neither crow nor crane." He was astonished; still he had to wait. At last the woman came, and he fell at her feet and said, "Mother, how did you know that?" She said, "My boy, I do not know your Yoga or your practices. I am a common everyday woman. I made you wait because my husband is ill, and I was nursing him. All my life I have struggled to do my duty. When I was unmarried, I did my duty to my parents; now that I am married, I do my duty to my husband; that is all the Yoga I practice. But by doing my duty I have become illumined; thus I could read your thoughts and know what you had done in the forest. If you want to know something higher than this, go to the market of such and such a town where you will find a Vyâdha (The lowest class of people in India who used to live as hunters and butchers.) who will tell you something that you will be very glad to learn." The Sannyasin thought, "Why should I go to that town and to a Vyadha?" But after what he had seen, his mind opened a little, so he went. When he came near the town, he found the market and there saw, at a distance, a big fat Vyadha cutting meat with big knives, talking and bargaining with different people. The young man said, "Lord help me! Is this the man from whom I am going to learn? He is the incarnation of a demon, if he is anything." In the meantime this man looked up and said, "O Swami, did that lady send you here? Take a seat until I have done my business." The Sannyasin thought, "What comes to me here?" He took his seat; the man went on with his work, and after he had finished he took his money and said to the Sannyasin, "Come sir, come to my home." On reaching home the Vyadha gave him a seat, saying, "Wait here," and went into the house. He then washed his old father and mother, fed them, and did all he could to please them, after which he came to the Sannyasin and said, "Now, sir, you have come here to see me; what can I do for you?" The Sannyasin asked him a few questions about soul and about God, and the Vyadha gave him a lecture which forms a part of the Mahâbhârata, called the *Vyâdha-Gitâ*. It contains one of the highest flights of the Vedanta. When the Vyadha finished his teaching, the Sannyasin felt astonished. He said, "Why are you in that body? With such knowledge as yours why are you in a Vyadha's body, and doing such filthy, ugly work?" "My son," replied the Vyadha, "no duty is ugly, no duty is impure. My birth placed me in these circumstances and environments. In my boyhood I learnt the trade; I am unattached, and I try to do my duty well. I try to do my duty as a householder, and I try to do all I can to make my father and mother happy. I neither know your Yoga, nor have I become a Sannyasin, nor did I go out of the world into a forest; nevertheless, all that you have heard and seen has come to me through the unattached doing of the duty which belongs to my position."

There is a sage in India, a great Yogi, one of the most wonderful men I have ever seen in my life. He is a peculiar man, he will not teach any one; if you ask him a question he will not answer. It is too much for him to take up the position of a teacher, he will not do it. If you ask a question, and wait for some days, in the course of conversation he will bring up the subject, and wonderful light will he throw on it. He told me once the secret of work, "Let the end and the means be joined into one." When you are doing any work, do not think of anything beyond. Do it as worship, as the highest worship, and devote your whole life to it for the time being. Thus, in the story, the Vyadha and the woman did their duty with cheerfulness and whole-heartedness; and the result was that they became illuminated, clearly showing that the right performance of the duties of any station in life, without attachment to results, leads us to the highest realisation of the perfection of the soul.

It is the worker who is attached to results that grumbles about the nature of the duty which has fallen to his lot; to the unattached worker all duties are equally good, and form efficient instruments with which selfishness and sensuality may be killed, and the freedom of the soul secured. We are all apt to think too highly of ourselves. Our duties are determined by our desires to a much larger extent than we are willing to grant. Competition rouses envy, and it kills the kindliness of the heart. To the grumbler all duties are distasteful; nothing will ever satisfy him, and his whole life is doomed to prove a failure. Let us work on, doing as we go whatever happens to be our duty, and being ever ready to put our shoulders to the wheel. Then surely shall we see the Light!

CHAPTER V
We Help Ourselves, Not The World

Before considering further how devotion to duty helps us in our spiritual progress, let me place before you in a brief compass another aspect of what we in India mean by Karma. In every religion there are three parts: philosophy, mythology, and ritual. Philosophy of course is the essence of every religion; mythology explains and illustrates it by means of the more or less legendary lives of great men, stories and fables of wonderful things, and so on; ritual gives to that philosophy a still more concrete form, so that every one may grasp it — ritual is in fact concretised philosophy. This ritual is Karma; it is necessary in every religion, because most of us cannot understand abstract spiritual things until we grow much spiritually. It is easy for men to think that they can understand anything; but when it comes to practical experience, they find that abstract ideas are often very hard to comprehend. Therefore symbols are of great help, and we cannot dispense with the symbolical method of putting things before us. From time immemorial symbols have been used by all kinds of religions. In one sense we cannot think but in symbols; words themselves are symbols of thought. In another sense everything in the universe may be looked upon as a symbol. The whole universe is a symbol, and God is the essence behind. This kind of symbology is not simply the creation of man; it is not that certain people belonging to a religion sit down together and think out certain symbols, and bring them into existence out of their own minds. The symbols of religion have a natural growth. Otherwise, why is it that certain symbols are associated with certain ideas in the mind of almost every one? Certain symbols are universally prevalent. Many of you may think that the cross first came into existence as a symbol in connection with the Christian religion, but as a matter of fact it existed before Christianity was, before Moses was born, before the Vedas were given out, before there was any human record of human things. The cross may be found to have been in existence among the Aztecs and the Phoenicians; every race seems to have had the cross. Again, the symbol of the crucified Saviour, of a man crucified upon a cross, appears to have been known to almost every nation. The circle has been a great symbol throughout the world. Then there is the most universal of all symbols, the Swastika. At one time it was thought that the Buddhists carried it all over the world with them, but it has been found out that ages before Buddhism it was used among nations. In Old Babylon and in Egypt it was to be found. What does this show? All these symbols could not have been purely conventional. There must be some reason for them; some natural association between them and the human mind. Language is not the result of convention; it is not that people ever agreed to represent certain ideas by certain words; there never was an idea without a corresponding word or a word without a corresponding idea; ideas and words are in their nature inseparable. The symbols to represent ideas may be sound symbols or colour symbols. Deaf and dumb people have to think with other than sound symbols. Every thought in the mind has a form as its counterpart. This is called in Sanskrit philosophy Nâma-Rupa — name and form. It is as impossible to create by convention a system of symbols as it is to create a language. In the world's ritualistic symbols we have an expression of the religious thought of humanity. It is easy to say that there is no use of rituals and temples and all such paraphernalia; every baby says that in modern times. But it must be easy for all to see that those who worship inside a temple are in many respects different from those who will not worship there. Therefore the association of particular temples, rituals, and other concrete forms with particular religions has a tendency to bring into the minds of the followers of those religions the thoughts for which those concrete things stand as symbols; and it is not wise to ignore rituals and symbology altogether. The study and practice of these things form naturally a part of Karma-Yoga.

There are many other aspects of this science of work. One among them is to know the relation between thought and word and what can be achieved by the power of the word. In every religion the power of the word is recognised, so much so that in some of them creation itself is said to have come out of the word. The external aspect of the thought of God is the Word, and as God thought and willed before He created, creation came out of the Word. In this stress and hurry of our materialistic life, our nerves lose sensibility and become hardened. The older we grow, the longer we are knocked about in the world, the more callous we become; and we are apt to neglect things that even happen persistently and prominently around us. Human nature, however, asserts itself sometimes, and we are led to inquire into and wonder at some of these common occurrences; wondering thus is the first step in the acquisition of light. Apart from the higher philosophic and religious value of the Word, we may see that sound symbols play a prominent part in the drama of human life. I am talking to you. I am not touching you; the pulsations of the air caused by my speaking go into your ear, they touch your nerves and produce effects in your minds. You cannot resist this. What can be more wonderful than this? One man calls another a fool, and at this the other stands up and clenches his fist and lands a blow on his nose. Look at the power of the word! There is a woman weeping and miserable; another woman comes along and speaks to her a few gentle words, the doubled up frame of the weeping woman becomes straightened at once, her sorrow is gone and she already begins to smile. Think of the power of words! They are a great force in higher philosophy as well as in common life. Day and night we manipulate this force without thought and without inquiry. To know the nature of this force and to use it well is also a part of Karma-Yoga.

Our duty to others means helping others; doing good to the world. Why should we do good to the world? Apparently to help the world, but really to help ourselves. We should always try to help the world, that should be the highest motive in us; but if we consider well, we find that the world does not require our help at all. This world was not made that you or I should come and help it. I once read a sermon in which it was said, "All this beautiful world is very good, because it gives us time and opportunity to help others." Apparently, this is a very beautiful sentiment, but is it not a blasphemy to say that the world needs our help? We cannot deny that there is much misery in it; to go out and help others is, therefore, the best thing we can do, although in the long run, we shall find that helping others is only helping ourselves. As a boy I had some white mice. They were kept in a little box in which there were little wheels, and when the mice tried to cross the wheels, the wheels turned and turned, and the mice never got anywhere. So it is with the world and our helping it. The only help is that we get moral exercise. This world is neither good nor evil; each man manufactures a world for himself. If a blind man begins to think of the world, it is either as soft or hard, or as cold or hot. We are a mass of happiness or misery; we have seen that hundreds of times in our lives. As a rule, the young are optimistic and the old pessimistic. The young have life before them; the old complain their day is gone; hundreds of desires, which they cannot fulfil struggle in their hearts. Both are foolish nevertheless. Life is good or evil according to the state of mind in which we look at it, it is neither by itself. Fire, by itself, is neither good nor evil. When it keeps us warm we say, "How beautiful is fire!" When it burns our fingers, we blame it. Still, in itself it is neither good nor bad. According as we use it, it produces in us the feeling of good or bad; so also is this world. It is perfect. By perfection is meant that it is perfectly fitted to meet its ends. We may all be perfectly sure that it will go on beautifully well without us, and we need not bother our heads wishing to help it.

Yet we must do good; the desire to do good is the highest motive power we have, if we know all the time that it is a privilege to help others. Do not stand on a high pedestal and take five cents in your hand and say, "Here, my poor man," but be grateful that the poor man is there, so that by making a gift to him you are able to help yourself. It is not the receiver that is blessed, but it is the giver. Be thankful that you are allowed to exercise your power of benevolence and mercy in the world, and thus become pure and perfect. All good acts tend to make us pure and perfect. What can we do at best? Build a hospital, make roads, or erect charity asylums. We may organise a charity and collect two or three millions of dollars, build a hospital with one million, with the second give balls and drink champagne, and of the third let the officers steal half, and leave the rest finally to reach the poor; but what are all these? One mighty wind in five minutes can break all your buildings up. What shall we do then? One volcanic eruption may sweep away all our roads and hospitals and cities and buildings. Let us give up all this foolish talk of doing good to the world. It is not waiting for your or my help; yet we must work and constantly do good, because it is a blessing to ourselves. That is the only way we can become perfect. No beggar whom we have helped has ever owed a single cent to us; we owe everything to him, because he has allowed us to exercise our charity on him. It is entirely wrong to think that we have done, or can do, good to the world, or to think that we have helped such and such people. It is a foolish thought, and all foolish thoughts bring misery. We think that we have helped some man and expect him to thank us, and because he does not, unhappiness comes to us. Why should we expect anything in return for what we do? Be grateful to the man you help, think of him as God. Is it not a great privilege to be allowed to worship God by helping our fellow men? If we were really unattached, we should escape all this pain of vain expectation, and could cheerfully do good work in the world. Never will unhappiness or misery come through work done without attachment. The world will go on with its happiness and misery through eternity.

There was a poor man who wanted some money; and somehow he had heard that if he could get hold of a ghost, he might command him to bring money or anything else he liked; so he was very anxious to get hold of a ghost. He went about searching for a man who would give him a ghost, and at last he found a sage with great powers, and besought his help. The sage asked him what he would do with a ghost. I want a ghost to work for me; teach me how to get hold of one, sir; I desire it very much," replied the man. But the sage said, "Don't disturb yourself, go home." The next day the man went again to the sage and began to weep and pray, "Give me a ghost; I must have a ghost, sir, to help me." At last the sage was disgusted, and said, "Take this charm, repeat this magic word, and a ghost will come, and whatever you say to him he will do. But beware; they are terrible beings, and must be kept continually busy. If you fail to give him work, he will take your life." The man replied, "That is easy; I can give him work for all his life." Then he went to a forest, and after long repetition of the magic word, a huge ghost appeared before him, and said, "I am a ghost. I have been conquered by your magic; but you must keep me constantly employed. The moment you fail to give me work I will kill you." The man said, "Build me a palace," and the ghost said, "It is done; the palace is built." "Bring me money," said the man. "Here is your money," said the ghost. "Cut this forest down, and build a city in its place." "That is done," said the ghost, "anything more?" Now the man began to be frightened and thought he could give him nothing more to do; he did everything in a trice. The ghost said, "Give me something to do or I will eat you up." The poor man could find no further occupation for him, and was frightened. So he ran and ran and at last reached the sage, and said, "Oh, sir, protect my life!" The sage asked him what the matter was, and the man replied, "I have nothing to give the ghost to do. Everything I tell him to do he does in a moment, and he threatens to eat me up if I do not give him work." Just then the ghost arrived, saying, "I'll eat you up," and he would have swallowed the man. The man began to shake, and begged the sage to save his life. The sage said, "I will find you a way out. Look at that dog with a curly tail. Draw your sword quickly and cut the tail off and give it to the ghost to straighten out." The man cut off the dog's tail and gave it to the ghost, saying, "Straighten that out for me." The ghost took it and slowly and carefully straightened it out, but as soon as he let it go, it instantly curled up again. Once more he laboriously straightened it out, only to find it again curled up as soon as he attempted to let go of it. Again he patiently straightened it out, but as soon as he let it go, it curled up again. So he went on for days and days, until he was exhausted and said, "I was never in such trouble before in my life. I am an old veteran ghost, but never before was I in such trouble." "I will make a compromise with you ;" he said to the man, "you let me off and I will let you keep all I have given you and will promise not to harm you." The man was much pleased, and accepted the offer gladly.

This world is like a dog's curly tail, and people have been striving to straighten it out for hundreds of years; but when they let it go, it has curled up again. How could it be otherwise? One must first know how to work without attachment, then one will not be a fanatic. When we know that this world is like a dog's curly tail and will never get straightened, we shall not become fanatics. If there were no fanaticism in the world, it would make much more progress than it does now. It is a mistake to think that fanaticism can make for the progress of mankind. On the contrary, it is a retarding element creating hatred and anger, and causing people to fight each other, and making them unsympathetic. We think that whatever we do or possess is the best in the world, and what we do not do or possess is of no value. So, always remember the instance of the curly tail of the dog whenever you have a tendency to become a fanatic. You need not worry or make yourself sleepless about the world; it will go on without you. When you have avoided fanaticism, then alone will you work well. It is the level-headed man, the calm man, of good judgment and cool nerves, of great sympathy and love, who does good work and so does good to himself. The fanatic is foolish and has no sympathy; he can never straighten the world, nor himself become pure and perfect.

To recapitulate the chief points in today's lecture: First, we have to bear in mind that we are all debtors to the world and the world does not owe us anything. It is a great privilege for all of us to be allowed to do anything for the world. In helping the world we really help ourselves. The second point is that there is a God in this universe. It is not true that this universe is drifting and stands in need of help from you and me. God is ever present therein, He is undying and eternally active and infinitely watchful. When the whole universe sleeps, He sleeps not; He is working incessantly; all the changes and manifestations of the world are His. Thirdly, we ought not to hate anyone. This world will always continue to be a mixture of good and evil. Our duty is to sympathise with the weak and to love even the wrongdoer. The world is a grand moral gymnasium wherein we have all to take exercise so as to become stronger and stronger spiritually. Fourthly, we ought not to be fanatics of any kind, because fanaticism is opposed to love. You hear fanatics glibly saying, "I do not hate the sinner. I hate the sin," but I am prepared to go any distance to see the face of that man who can really make a distinction between the sin and the sinner. It is easy to say so. If we can distinguish well between quality and substance, we may become perfect men. It is not easy to do this. And further, the calmer we are and the less disturbed our nerves, the more shall we love and the better will our work be.

CHAPTER VI
Non-Attachment is Complete Self-Abnegation

Just as every action that emanates from us comes back to us as reaction, even so our actions may act on other people and theirs on us. Perhaps all of you have observed it as a fact that when persons do evil actions, they become more and more evil, and when they begin to do good, they become stronger and stronger and learn to do good at all times. This intensification of the influence of action cannot be explained on any other ground than that we can act and react upon each other. To take an illustration from physical science, when I am doing a certain action, my mind may be said to be in a certain state of vibration; all minds which are in similar circumstances will have the tendency to be affected by my mind. If there are different musical instruments tuned alike in one room, all of you may have noticed that when one is struck, the others have the tendency to vibrate so as to give the same note. So all minds that have the same tension, so to say, will be equally affected by the same thought. Of course, this influence of thought on mind will vary according to distance and other causes, but the mind is always open to affection. Suppose I am doing an evil act, my mind is in a certain state of vibration, and all minds in the universe, which are in a similar state, have the possibility of being affected by the vibration of my mind. So, when I am doing a good action, my mind is in another state of vibration; and all minds similarly strung have the possibility of being affected by my mind; and this power of mind upon mind is more or less according as the force of the tension is greater or less.

Following this simile further, it is quite possible that, just as light waves may travel for millions of years before they reach any object, so thought waves may also travel hundreds of years before they meet an object with which they vibrate in unison. It is quite possible, therefore, that this atmosphere of ours is full of such thought pulsations, both good and evil. Every thought projected from every brain goes on pulsating, as it were, until it meets a fit object that will receive it. Any mind which is open to receive some of these impulses will take them immediately. So, when a man is doing evil actions, he has brought his mind to a certain state of tension and all the waves which correspond to that state of tension, and which may be said to be already in the atmosphere, will struggle to enter into his mind. That is why an evil-doer generally goes on doing more and more evil. His actions become intensified. Such, also will be the case with the doer of good; he will open himself to all the good waves that are in the atmosphere, and his good actions also will become intensified. We run, therefore, a twofold danger in doing evil: first, we open ourselves to all the evil influences surrounding us; secondly, we create evil which affects others, may be hundreds of years hence. In doing evil we injure ourselves and others also. In doing good we do good to ourselves and to others as well; and, like all other forces in man, these forces of good and evil also gather strength from outside.

According to Karma-Yoga, the action one has done cannot be destroyed until it has borne its fruit; no power in nature can stop it from yielding its results. If I do an evil action, I must suffer for it; there is no power in this universe to stop or stay it. Similarly, if I do a good action, there is no power in the universe which can stop its bearing good results. The cause must have its effect; nothing can prevent or restrain this. Now comes a very fine and serious question about Karma-Yoga — namely, that these actions of ours, both good and evil, are intimately connected with each other. We cannot put a line of demarcation and say, this action is entirely good and this entirely evil. There is no action which does not bear good and evil fruits at the same time. To take the nearest example: I am talking to you, and some of you, perhaps, think I am doing good; and at the same time I am, perhaps, killing thousands of microbes in the atmosphere; I am thus doing evil to something else. When it is very near to us and affects those we know, we say that it is very good action if it affects them in a good manner. For instance, you may call my speaking to you very good, but the microbes will not; the microbes you do not see, but yourselves you do see. The way in which my talk affects you is obvious to you, but how it affects the microbes is not so obvious. And so, if we analyse our evil actions also, we may find that some good possibly results from them somewhere. He who in good action sees that there is something evil in it, and in the midst of evil sees that there is something good in it somewhere, has known the secret of work.

But what follows from it? That, howsoever we may try, there cannot be any action which is perfectly pure, or any which is perfectly impure, taking purity and impurity in the sense of injury and non-injury. We cannot breathe or live without injuring others, and every bit of the food we eat is taken away from another's mouth. Our very lives are crowding out other lives. It may be men, or animals, or small microbes, but some one or other of these we have to crowd out. That being the case, it naturally follows that perfection can never be attained by work. We may work through all eternity, but there will be no way out of this intricate maze. You may work on, and on, and on; there will be no end to this inevitable association of good and evil in the results of work.

The second point to consider is, what is the end of work? We find the vast majority of people in every country believing that there will be a time when this world will become perfect, when there will be no disease, nor death, nor unhappiness, nor wickedness. That is a very good idea, a very good motive power to inspire and uplift the ignorant; but if we think for a moment, we shall find on the very face of it that it cannot be so. How can it be, seeing that good and evil are the obverse and reverse of the same coin? How can you have good without evil at the same time? What is meant by perfection? A perfect life is a contradiction in terms. Life itself is a state of continuous struggle between ourselves and everything outside. Every moment we are fighting actually with external nature, and if we are defeated, our life has to go. It is, for instance, a continuous struggle for food and air. If food or air fails, we die. Life is not a simple and smoothly flowing thing, but it is a compound effect. This complex struggle between something inside and the external world is what we call life. So it is clear that when this struggle ceases, there will be an end of life.

What is meant by ideal happiness is the cessation of this struggle. But then life will cease, for the struggle can only cease when life itself has ceased. We have seen already that in helping the world we help ourselves. The main effect of work done for others is to purify ourselves. By means of the constant effort to do good to others we are trying to forget ourselves; this forgetfulness of self is the one great lesson we have to learn in life. Man thinks foolishly that he can make himself happy, and after years of struggle finds out at last that true happiness consists in killing selfishness and that no one can make him happy except himself. Every act of charity, every thought of sympathy, every action of help, every good deed, is taking so much of self-importance away from our little selves and making us think of ourselves as the lowest and the least, and, therefore, it is all good. Here we find that Jnâna, Bhakti, and Karma — all come to one point. The highest ideal is eternal and entire self-abnegation, where there is no "I," but all is "Thou"; and whether he is conscious or unconscious of it, Karma-Yoga leads man to that end. A religious preacher may become horrified at the idea of an Impersonal God; he may insist on a Personal God and wish to keep up his own identity and individuality, whatever he may mean by that. But his ideas of ethics, if they are really good, cannot but be based on the highest self-abnegation. It is the basis of all morality; you may extend it to men, or animals, or angels, it is the one basic idea, the one fundamental principle running through all ethical systems.

You will find various classes of men in this world. First, there are the God-men, whose self-abnegation is complete, and who do only good to others even at the sacrifice of their own lives. These are the highest of men. If there are a hundred of such in any country, that country need never despair. But they are unfortunately too few. Then there are the good men who do good to others so long as it does not injure themselves. And there is a third class who, to do good to themselves, injure others. It is said by a Sanskrit poet that there is a fourth unnamable class of people who injure others merely for injury's sake. Just as there are at one pole of existence the highest good men, who do good for the sake of doing good, so, at the other pole, there are others who injure others just for the sake of the injury. They do not gain anything thereby, but it is their nature to do evil.

Here are two Sanskrit words. The one is Pravritti, which means revolving towards, and the other is Nivritti, which means revolving away. The "revolving towards" is what we call the world, the "I and mine"; it includes all those things which are always enriching that "me" by wealth and money and power, and name and fame, and which are of a grasping nature, always tending to accumulate everything in one centre, that centre being "myself". That is the Pravritti, the natural tendency of every human being; taking everything from everywhere and heaping it around one centre, that centre being man's own sweet self. When this tendency begins to break, when it is Nivritti or "going away from," then begin morality and religion. Both Pravritti and Nivritti are of the nature of work: the former is evil work, and the latter is good work. This Nivritti is the fundamental basis of all morality and all religion, and the very perfection of it is entire self-abnegation, readiness to sacrifice mind and body and everything for another being. When a man has reached that state, he has attained to the perfection of Karma-Yoga. This is the highest result of good works. Although a man has not studied a single system of philosophy, although he does not believe in any God, and never has believed, although he has not prayed even once in his whole life, if the simple power of good actions has brought him to that state where he is ready to give up his life and all else for others, he has arrived at the same point to which the religious man will come through his prayers and the philosopher through his knowledge; and so you may find that the philosopher, the worker, and the devotee, all meet at one point, that one point being self-abnegation. However much their systems of philosophy and religion may differ, all mankind stand in reverence and awe before the man who is ready to sacrifice himself for others. Here, it is not at all any question of creed, or doctrine — even men who are very much opposed to all religious ideas, when they see one of these acts of complete self-sacrifice, feel that they must revere it. Have you not seen even a most bigoted Christian, when he reads Edwin Arnold's *Light of Asia*, stand in reverence of Buddha, who Preached no God, preached nothing but self-sacrifice? The only thing is that the bigot does not know that his own end and aim in life is exactly the same as that of those from whom he differs. The worshipper, by keeping constantly before him the idea of God and a surrounding of good, comes to the same point at last and says, "Thy will be done," and keeps nothing to himself. That is self-abnegation. The philosopher, with his knowledge, sees that the seeming self is a delusion and easily gives it up. It is self-abnegation. So Karma, Bhakti, and Jnana all meet here; and this is what was meant by all the great preachers of ancient times, when they taught that God is not the world. There is one thing which is the world and another which is God; and this distinction is very true. What they mean by world is selfishness. Unselfishness is God. One may live on a throne, in a golden palace, and be perfectly unselfish; and then he is in God. Another may live in a hut and wear rags, and have nothing in the world; yet, if he is selfish, he is intensely merged in the world.

To come back to one of our main points, we say that we cannot do good without at the same time doing some evil, or do evil without doing some good. Knowing this, how can we work? There have, therefore, been sects in this world who have in an astoundingly preposterous way preached slow suicide as the only means to get out of the world, because if a man lives, he has to kill poor little animals and plants or do injury to something or some one. So according to them the only way out of the world is to die. The Jains have preached this doctrine as their highest ideal. This teaching seems to be very logical. But the true solution is found in the Gita. It is the theory of non-attachment, to be attached to nothing while doing our work of life. Know that you are separated entirely from the world, though you are in the world, and that whatever you may be doing in it, you are not doing that for your own sake. Any action that you do for yourself will bring its effect to bear upon you. If it is a good action, you will have to take the good effect, and if bad, you will have to take the bad effect; but any action that is not done for your own sake, whatever it be, will have no effect on you. There is to be found a very expressive sentence in our scriptures embodying this idea: "Even if he kill the whole universe (or be himself killed), he is neither the killer nor the killed, when he knows that he is not acting for himself at all." Therefore Karma-Yoga teaches, "Do not give up the world; live in the world, imbibe its influences as much as you can; but if it be for your own enjoyment's sake, work not at all." Enjoyment should not be the goal. First kill your self and then take the whole world as yourself; as the old Christians used to say, "The old man must die." This old man is the selfish idea that the whole world is made for our enjoyment. Foolish parents teach their children to pray, "O Lord, Thou hast created this sun for me and this moon for me," as if the Lord has had nothing else to do than to create everything for these babies. Do not teach your children such nonsense. Then again, there are people who are foolish in another way: they teach us that all these animals were created for us to kill and eat, and that this universe is for the enjoyment of men. That is all foolishness. A tiger may say, "Man was created for me" and pray, "O Lord, how wicked are these men who do not come and place themselves before me to be eaten; they are breaking Your law." If the world is created for us, we are also created for the world. That this world is created for our enjoyment is the most wicked idea that holds us down. This world is not for our sake. Millions pass out of it every year; the world does not feel it; millions of others are supplied in their place. Just as much as the world is for us, so we also are for the world.

To work properly, therefore, you have first to give up the idea of attachment. Secondly, do not mix in the fray, hold yourself as a witness and go on working. My master used to say, "Look upon your children as a nurse does." The nurse will take your baby and fondle it and play with it and behave towards it as gently as if it were her own child; but as soon as you give her notice to quit, she is ready to start off bag and baggage from the house. Everything in the shape of attachment is forgotten; it will not give the ordinary nurse the least pang to leave your children and take up other children. Even so are you to be with all that you consider your own. You are the nurse, and if you believe in God, believe that all these things which you consider yours are really His. The greatest weakness often insinuates itself as the greatest good and strength. It is a weakness to think that any one is dependent on me, and that I can do good to another. This belief is the mother of all our attachment, and through this attachment comes all our pain. We must inform our minds that no one in this universe depends upon us; not one beggar depends on our charity; not one soul on our kindness; not one living thing on our help. All are helped on by nature, and will be so helped even though millions of us were not here. The course of nature will not stop for such as you and me; it is, as already pointed out, only a blessed privilege to you and to me that we are allowed, in the way of helping others, to educate ourselves. This is a great lesson to learn in life, and when we have learned it fully, we shall never be unhappy; we can go and mix without harm in society anywhere and everywhere. You may have wives and husbands, and regiments of servants, and kingdoms to govern; if only you act on the principle that the world is not for you and does not inevitably need you, they can do you no harm. This very year some of your friends may have died. Is the world waiting without going on, for them to come again? Is its current stopped? No, it goes on. So drive out of your mind the idea that you have to do something for the world; the world does not require any help from you. It is sheer nonsense on the part of any man to think that he is born to help the world; it is simply pride, it is selfishness insinuating itself in the form of virtue. When you have trained your mind and your nerves to realise this idea of the world's non-dependence on you or on anybody, there will then be no reaction in the form of pain resulting from work. When you give something to a man and expect nothing — do not even expect the man to be grateful — his ingratitude will not tell upon you, because you never expected anything, never thought you had any right to anything in the way of a return. You gave him what he deserved; his own Karma got it for him; your Karma made you the carrier thereof. Why should you be proud of having given away something? You are the porter that carried the money or other kind of gift, and the world deserved it by its own Karma. Where is then the reason for pride in you? There is nothing very great in what you give to the world. When you have acquired the feeling of non-attachment, there will then be neither good nor evil for you. It is only selfishness that causes the difference between good and evil. It is a very hard thing to understand, but you will come to learn in time that nothing in the universe has power over you until you allow it to exercise such a power. Nothing has power over the Self of man, until the Self becomes a fool and loses independence. So, by non-attachment, you overcome and deny the power of anything to act upon you. It is very easy to say that nothing has the right to act upon you until you allow it to do so; but what is the true sign of the man who really does not allow anything to work upon him, who is neither happy nor unhappy when acted upon by the external world? The sign is that good or ill fortune causes no change in his mind: in all conditions he continues to remain the same.

There was a great sage in India called Vyâsa. This Vyâsa is known as the author of the Vedanta aphorisms, and was a holy man. His father had tried to become a very perfect man and had failed. His grandfather had also tried and failed. His great-grandfather had similarly tried and failed. He himself did not succeed perfectly, but his son, Shuka, was born perfect. Vyasa taught his son wisdom; and after teaching him the knowledge of truth himself, he sent him to the court of King Janaka. He was a great king and was called Janaka Videha. Videha means "without a body". Although a king, he had entirely forgotten that he was a body; he felt that he was a spirit all the time. This boy Shuka was sent to be taught by him. The king knew that Vyasa's son was coming to him to learn wisdom: so he made certain arrangements beforehand. And when the boy presented himself at the gates of the palace, the guards took no notice of him whatsoever. They only gave him a seat, and he sat there for three days and nights, nobody speaking to him, nobody asking him who he was or whence he was. He was the son of a very great sage, his father was honoured by the whole country, and he himself was a most respectable person; yet the low, vulgar guards of the palace would take no notice of him. After that, suddenly, the ministers of the king and all the big officials came there and received him with the greatest honours. They conducted him in and showed him into splendid rooms, gave him the most fragrant baths and wonderful dresses, and for eight days they kept him there in all kinds of luxury. That solemnly serene face of Shuka did not change even to the smallest extent by the change in the treatment accorded to him; he was the same in the midst of this luxury as when waiting at the door. Then he was brought before the king. The king was on his throne, music was playing, and dancing and other amusements were going on. The king then gave him a cup of milk, full to the brim, and asked him to go seven times round the hall without spilling even a drop. The boy took the cup and proceeded in the midst of the music and the attraction of the beautiful faces. As desired by the king, seven times did he go round, and not a drop of the milk was spilt. The boy's mind could not be attracted by anything in the world, unless he allowed it to affect him. And when he brought the cup to the king, the king said to him, "What your father has taught you, and what you have learned yourself, I can only repeat. You have known the Truth; go home."

Thus the man that has practiced control over himself cannot be acted upon by anything outside; there is no more slavery for him. His mind has become free. Such a man alone is fit to live well in the world. We generally find men holding two opinions regarding the world. Some are pessimists and say, "How horrible this world is, how wicked!" Some others are optimists and say, "How beautiful this world is, how wonderful!" To those who have not controlled their own minds, the world is either full of evil or at best a mixture of good and evil. This very world will become to us an optimistic world when we become masters of our own minds. Nothing will then work upon us as good or evil; we shall find everything to be in its proper place, to be harmonious. Some men, who begin by saying that the world is a hell, often end by saying that it is a heaven when they succeed in the practice of self-control. If we are genuine Karma-Yogis and wish to train ourselves to that attainment of this state, wherever we may begin we are sure to end in perfect self-abnegation; and as soon as this seeming self has gone, the whole world, which at first appears to us to be filled with evil, will appear to be heaven itself and full of blessedness. Its very atmosphere will be blessed; every human face there will be god. Such is the end and aim of Karma-Yoga, and such is its perfection in practical life.

Our various Yogas do not conflict with each other; each of them leads us to the same goal and makes us perfect. Only each has to be strenuously practiced. The whole secret is in practicing. First you have to hear, then think, and then practice. This is true of every Yoga. You have first to hear about it and understand what it is; and many things which you do not understand will be made clear to you by constant hearing and thinking. It is hard to understand everything at once. The explanation of everything is after all in yourself. No one was ever really taught by another; each of us has to teach himself. The external teacher offers only the suggestion which rouses the internal teacher to work to understand things. Then things will be made clearer to us by our own power of perception and thought, and we shall realise them in our own souls; and that realisation will grow into the intense power of will. First it is feeling, then it becomes willing, and out of that willing comes the tremendous force for work that will go through every vein and nerve and muscle, until the whole mass of your body is changed into an instrument of the unselfish Yoga of work, and the desired result of perfect self-abnegation and utter unselfishness is duly attained. This attainment does not depend on any dogma, or doctrine, or belief. Whether one is Christian, or Jew, or Gentile, it does not matter. Are you unselfish? That is the question. If you are, you will be perfect without reading a single religious book, without going into a single church or temple. Each one of our Yogas is fitted to make man perfect even without the help of the others, because they have all the same goal in view. The Yogas of work, of wisdom, and of devotion are all capable of serving as direct and independent means for the attainment of Moksha. "Fools alone say that work and philosophy are different, not the learned." The learned know that, though apparently different from each other, they at last lead to the same goal of human perfection.

CHAPTER VII
Freedom

In addition to meaning work, we have stated that psychologically the word Karma also implies causation. Any work, any action, any thought that produces an effect is called a Karma. Thus the law of Karma means the law of causation, of inevitable cause and sequence. Wheresoever there is a cause, there an effect must be produced; this necessity cannot be resisted, and this law of Karma, according to our philosophy, is true throughout the whole universe. Whatever we see, or feel, or do, whatever action there is anywhere in the universe, while being the effect of past work on the one hand, becomes, on the other, a cause in its turn, and produces its own effect. It is necessary, together with this, to consider what is meant by the word "law". By law is meant the tendency of a series to repeat itself. When we see one event followed by another, or sometimes happening simultaneously with another, we expect this sequence or co-existence to recur. Our old logicians and philosophers of the Nyâyâ school call this law by the name of Vyâpti. According to them, all our ideas of law are due to association. A series of phenomena becomes associated with things in our mind in a sort of invariable order, so that whatever we perceive at any time is immediately referred to other facts in the mind. Any one idea or, according to our psychology, any one wave that is produced in the mind-stuff, Chitta, must always give rise to many similar waves. This is the psychological idea of association, and causation is only an aspect of this grand pervasive principle of association. This pervasiveness of association is what is, in Sanskrit, called Vyâpti. In the external world the idea of law is the same as in the internal — the expectation that a particular phenomenon will be followed by another, and that the series will repeat itself. Really speaking, therefore, law does not exist in nature. Practically it is an error to say that gravitation exists in the earth, or that there is any law existing objectively anywhere in nature. Law is the method, the manner in which our mind grasps a series of phenomena; it is all in the mind. Certain phenomena, happening one after another or together, and followed by the conviction of the regularity of their recurrence — thus enabling our minds to grasp the method of the whole series — constitute what we call law.

The next question for consideration is what we mean by law being universal. Our universe is that portion of existence which is characterized by what the Sanskrit psychologists call Desha-kâla-nimitta, or what is known to European psychology as space, time, and causation. This universe is only a part of infinite existence, thrown into a peculiar mould, composed of space, time, and causation. It necessarily follows that law is possible only within this conditioned universe; beyond it there cannot be any law. When we speak of the universe, we only mean that portion of existence which is limited by our mind — the universe of the senses, which we can see, feel, touch, hear, think of, imagine. This alone is under law; but beyond it existence cannot be subject to law, because causation does not extend beyond the world of our minds. Anything beyond the range of our mind and our senses is not bound by the law of causation, as there is no mental association of things in the region beyond the senses, and no causation without association of ideas. It is only when "being" or existence gets moulded into name and form that it obeys the law of causation, and is said to be under law; because all law has its essence in causation. Therefore we see at once that there cannot be any such thing as free will; the very words are a contradiction, because will is what we know, and everything that we know is within our universe, and everything within our universe is moulded by the conditions of space, time, and causation. Everything that we know, or can possibly know, must be subject to causation, and that which obeys the law of causation cannot be free. It is acted upon by other agents, and becomes a cause in its turn. But that which has become converted into the will, which was not the will before, but which, when it fell into this mould of space, time, and causation, became converted into the human will, is free; and when this will gets out of this mould of space, time, and causation, it will be free again. From freedom it comes, and becomes moulded into this bondage, and it gets out and goes back to freedom again.

The question has been raised as to from whom this universe comes, in whom it rests, and to whom it goes; and the answer has been given that from freedom it comes, in bondage it rests, and goes back into that freedom again. So, when we speak of man as no other than that infinite being which is manifesting itself, we mean that only one very small part thereof is man; this body and this mind which we see are only one part of the whole, only one spot of the infinite being. This whole universe is only one speck of the infinite being; and all our laws, our bondages, our joys and our sorrows, our happinesses and our expectations, are only within this small universe; all our progression and digression are within its small compass. So you see how childish it is to expect a continuation of this universe — the creation of our minds — and to expect to go to heaven, which after all must mean only a repetition of this world that we know. You see at once that it is an impossible and childish desire to make the whole of infinite existence conform to the limited and conditioned existence which we know. When a man says that he will have again and again this same thing which he is hating now, or, as I sometimes put it, when he asks for a *comfortable* religion, you may know that he has become so degenerate that he cannot think of anything higher than what he is now; he is just his little present surroundings and nothing more. He has forgotten his infinite nature, and his whole idea is confined to these little joys, and sorrows, and heart-jealousies of the moment. He thinks that this finite thing is the infinite; and not only so, he will not let this foolishness go. He clings on desperately unto Trishnâ, and the thirst after life, what the Buddhists call Tanhâ and Tissâ. There may be millions of kinds of happiness, and beings, and laws, and progress, and causation, all acting outside the little universe that we know; and, after all, the whole of this comprises but one section of our infinite nature.

To acquire freedom we have to get beyond the limitations of this universe; it cannot be found here. Perfect equilibrium, or what the Christians call the peace that passeth all understanding, cannot be had in this universe, nor in heaven, nor in any place where our mind and thoughts can go, where the senses can feel, or which the imagination can conceive. No such place can give us that freedom, because all such places would be within our universe, and it is limited by space, time, and causation. There may be places that are more ethereal than this earth of ours, where enjoyments may be keener, but even those places must be in the universe and, therefore, in bondage to law; so we have to go beyond, and real religion begins where this little universe ends. These little joys, and sorrows, and knowledge of things end there, and the reality begins. Until we give up the thirst after life, the strong attachment to this our transient conditioned existence we have no hope of catching even a glimpse of that infinite freedom beyond. It stands to reason then that there is only one way to attain to that freedom which is the goal of all the noblest aspirations of mankind, and that is by giving up this little life, giving up this little universe, giving up this earth, giving up heaven, giving up the body, giving up the mind, giving up everything that is limited and conditioned. If we give up our attachment to this little universe of the senses or of the mind, we shall be free immediately. The only way to come out of bondage is to go beyond the limitations of law, to go beyond causation.

But it is a most difficult thing to give up the clinging to this universe; few ever attain to that. There are two ways to do that mentioned in our books. One is called the "Neti, Neti" (not this, not this), the other is called "Iti" (this); the former is the negative, and the latter is the positive way. The negative way is the most difficult. It is only possible to the men of the very highest, exceptional minds and gigantic wills who simply stand up and say, "No, I will not have this," and the mind and body obey their will, and they come out successful. But such people are very rare. The vast majority of mankind choose the positive way, the way through the world, making use of all the bondages themselves to break those very bondages. This is also a kind of giving up; only it is done slowly and gradually, by knowing things, enjoying things and thus obtaining experience, and knowing the nature of things until the mind lets them all go at last and becomes unattached. The former way of obtaining non-attachment is by reasoning, and the latter way is through work and experience. The first is the path of Jnâna-Yoga, and is characterized by the refusal to do any work; the second is that of Karma-Yoga, in which there is no cessation from work. Every one must work in the universe. Only those who are perfectly satisfied with the Self, whose desires do not go beyond the Self, whose mind never strays out of the Self, to whom the Self is all in all, only those do not work. The rest must work. A current rushing down of its own nature falls into a hollow and makes a whirlpool, and, after running a little in that whirlpool, it emerges again in the form of the free current to go on unchecked. Each human life is like that current. It gets into the whirl, gets involved in this world of space, time, and causation, whirls round a little, crying out, "my father, my brother, my name, my fame", and so on, and at last emerges out of it and regains its original freedom. The whole universe is doing that. Whether we know it or not, whether we are conscious or unconscious of it, we are all working to get out of the dream of the world. Man's experience in the world is to enable him to get out of its whirlpool.

What is Karma-Yoga? The knowledge of the secret of work. We see that the whole universe is working. For what? For salvation, for liberty; from the atom to the highest being, working for the one end, liberty for the mind, for the body, for the spirit. All things are always trying to get freedom, flying away from bondage. The sun, the moon, the earth, the planets, all are trying to fly away from bondage. The centrifugal and the centripetal forces of nature are indeed typical of our universe. Instead of being knocked about in this universe, and after long delay and thrashing, getting to know things as they are, we learn from Karma-Yoga the secret of work, the method of work, the organising power of work. A vast mass of energy may be spent in vain if we do not know how to utilise it. Karma-Yoga makes a science of work; you learn by it how best to utilise all the workings of this world. Work is inevitable, it must be so; but we should work to the highest purpose. Karma-Yoga makes us admit that this world is a world of five minutes, that it is a something we have to pass through; and that freedom is not here, but is only to be found beyond. To find the way out of the bondages of the world we have to go through it slowly and surely. There may be those exceptional persons about whom I just spoke, those who can stand aside and give up the world, as a snake casts off its skin and stands aside and looks at it. There are no doubt these exceptional beings; but the rest of mankind have to go slowly through the world of work. Karma-Yoga shows the process, the secret, and the method of doing it to the best advantage.

What does it say? "Work incessantly, but give up all attachment to work." Do not identify yourself with anything. Hold your mind free. All this that you see, the pains and the miseries, are but the necessary conditions of this world; poverty and wealth and happiness are but momentary; they do not belong to our real nature at all. Our nature is far beyond misery and happiness, beyond every object of the senses, beyond the imagination; and yet we must go on working all the time. "Misery comes through attachment, not through work." As soon as we identify ourselves with the work we do, we feel miserable; but if we do not identify ourselves with it, we do not feel that misery. If a beautiful picture belonging to another is burnt, a man does not generally become miserable; but when his own picture is burnt, how miserable he feels! Why? Both were beautiful pictures, perhaps copies of the same original; but in one case very much more misery is felt than in the other. It is because in one case he identifies himself with the picture, and not in the other. This "I and mine" causes the whole misery. With the sense of possession comes selfishness, and selfishness brings on misery. Every act of selfishness or thought of selfishness makes us attached to something, and immediately we are made slaves. Each wave in the Chitta that says "I and mine" immediately puts a chain round us and makes us slaves; and the more we say "I and mine", the more slavery grows, the more misery increases. Therefore Karma-Yoga tells us to enjoy the beauty of all the pictures in the world, but not to identify ourselves with any of them. Never say "mine". Whenever we say a thing is "mine", misery will immediately come. Do not even say "my child" in your mind. Possess the child, but do not say "mine". If you do, then will come the misery. Do not say "my house," do not say "my body". The whole difficulty is there. The body is neither yours, nor mine, nor anybody's. These bodies are coming and going by the laws of nature, but we are free, standing as witness. This body is no more free than a picture or a wall. Why should we be attached so much to a body? If somebody paints a picture, he does it and passes on. Do not project that tentacle of selfishness, "I must possess it". As soon as that is projected, misery will begin.

So Karma-Yoga says, first destroy the tendency to project this tentacle of selfishness, and when you have the power of checking it, hold it in and do not allow the mind to get into the ways of selfishness. Then you may go out into the world and work as much as you

can. Mix everywhere, go where you please; you will
never be contaminated with evil. There is the lotus leaf
in the water; the water cannot touch and adhere to it;
so will you be in the world. This is called "Vairâgya",
dispassion or non-attachment. I believe I have told you
that without non-attachment there cannot be any kind
of Yoga. Non-attachment is the basis of all the Yogas.
The man who gives up living in houses, wearing fine
clothes, and eating good food, and goes into the desert,
may be a most attached person. His only possession,
his own body, may become everything to him; and as
he lives he will be simply struggling for the sake of
his body. Non-attachment does not mean anything that
we may do in relation to our external body, it is all in
the mind. The binding link of "I and mine" is in the
mind. If we have not this link with the body and with
the things of the senses, we are non-attached, wherever
and whatever we may be. A man may be on a throne
and perfectly non-attached; another man may be in rags
and still very much attached. First, we have to attain this
state of non-attachment and then to work incessantly.
Karma-Yoga gives us the method that will help us in
giving up all attachment, though it is indeed very hard.

Here are the two ways of giving up all attachment.
The one is for those who do not believe in God, or in
any outside help. They are left to their own devices;
they have simply to work with their own will, with the
powers of their mind and discrimination, saying, "I

must be non-attached". For those who believe in God there is another way, which is much less difficult. They give up the fruits of work unto the Lord; they work and are never attached to the results. Whatever they see, feel, hear, or do, is for Him. For whatever good work we may do, let us not claim any praise or benefit. It is the Lord's; give up the fruits unto Him. Let us stand aside and think that we are only servants obeying the Lord, our Master, and that every impulse for action comes from Him every moment. Whatever thou worshippest, whatever thou perceivest, whatever thou doest, give up all unto Him and be at rest. Let us be at peace, perfect peace, with ourselves, and give up our whole body and mind and everything as an eternal sacrifice unto the Lord. Instead of the sacrifice of pouring oblations into the fire, perform this one great sacrifice day and night — the sacrifice of your little self. "In search of wealth in this world, Thou art the only wealth I have found; I sacrifice myself unto Thee. In search of some one to be loved, Thou art the only one beloved I have found; I sacrifice myself unto Thee." Let us repeat this day and night, and say, "Nothing for me; no matter whether the thing is good, bad, or indifferent; I do not care for it; I sacrifice all unto Thee." Day and night let us renounce our seeming self until it becomes a habit with us to do so, until it gets into the blood, the nerves, and the brain, and the whole body is every moment obedient to this idea of self-renunciation. Go then into the midst of the battlefield, with the roaring cannon and the din of war, and you will find yourself to be free and at peace.

Karma-Yoga teaches us that the ordinary idea of duty is on the lower plane; nevertheless, all of us have to do our duty. Yet we may see that this peculiar sense of duty is very often a great cause of misery. Duty becomes a disease with us; it drags us ever forward. It catches hold of us and makes our whole life miserable. It is the bane of human life. This duty, this idea of duty is the midday summer sun which scorches the innermost soul of mankind. Look at those poor slaves to duty! Duty leaves them no time to say prayers, no time to bathe. Duty is ever on them. They go out and work. Duty is on them! They come home and think of the work for the next day. Duty is on them! It is living a slave's life, at last dropping down in the street and dying in harness, like a horse. This is duty as it is understood. The only true duty is to be unattached and to work as free beings, to give up all work unto God. All our duties are His. Blessed are we that we are ordered out here. We serve our time; whether we do it ill or well, who knows? If we do it well, we do not get the fruits. If we do it ill, neither do we get the care. Be at rest, be free, and work. This kind of freedom is a very hard thing to attain. How easy it is to interpret slavery as duty — the morbid attachment of flesh for flesh as duty! Men go out into the world and struggle and fight for money or for any other thing to which they get attached. Ask them why they do it. They say, "It is a duty". It is the absurd greed for gold and gain, and they try to cover it with a few flowers.

What is duty after all? It is really the impulsion of the flesh, of our attachment; and when an attachment has become established, we call it duty. For instance, in countries where there is no marriage, there is no duty between husband and wife; when marriage comes, husband and wife live together on account of attachment; and that kind of living together becomes settled after generations; and when it becomes so settled, it becomes a duty. It is, so to say, a sort of chronic disease. When it is acute, we call it disease; when it is chronic, we call it nature. It is a disease. So when attachment becomes chronic, we baptise it with the high sounding name of duty. We strew flowers upon it, trumpets sound for it, sacred texts are said over it, and then the whole world fights, and men earnestly rob each other for this duty's sake. Duty is good to the extent that it checks brutality. To the lowest kinds of men, who cannot have any other ideal, it is of some good; but those who want to be Karma-Yogis must throw this idea of duty overboard. There is no duty for you and me. Whatever you have to give to the world, do give by all means, but not as a duty. Do not take any thought of that. Be not compelled. Why should you be compelled? *Everything that you do under compulsion goes to build up attachment.* Why should you have any duty? Resign everything unto God. In this tremendous fiery furnace where the fire of duty scorches everybody, drink this cup of nectar and be happy. We are all simply working out His will, and have nothing to do with rewards and punishments. If you want the reward, you must also have the punishment; the only way to get out of the punishment is to give up the reward. The only way of getting out of misery is by giving up the idea of happiness, because these two are linked to each other. On one side there is happiness, on the other there is misery. On one side there is life, on the other there is death. The only way to get beyond death is to give up the love of life. Life and death are the same thing, looked at from different points. So the idea of happiness without misery, or of life without death, is very good for school-boys and children; but the thinker sees that it is all a contradiction in terms and gives up both. Seek no praise, no reward, for anything you do. No sooner do we perform a good action than we begin to desire credit for it. No sooner do we give money to some charity than we want to see our names blazoned in the papers. Misery must come as the result of such desires. The greatest men in the world have passed away unknown. The Buddhas and the Christs that we know are but second-rate heroes in comparison with the greatest men of whom the world knows nothing. Hundreds of these unknown heroes have lived in every country working silently. Silently they live and silently they pass away; and in time their thoughts find expression in Buddhas or Christs, and it is these latter that become known to us. The highest men do not seek to get any name or fame from their knowledge. They leave their ideas to the world; they put forth no claims for themselves and establish no schools or systems in their name. Their whole nature shrinks from such a thing. They are the pure Sâttvikas, who can never make any stir, but only melt down in love. I have seen one such Yogi who lives in a cave in India. He is one of the most wonderful men I have ever seen. He has so completely lost the sense of his own individuality that we may say that the man in him is completely gone, leaving behind only the all comprehending sense of the divine. If an animal bites one of his arms, he is ready to give it his other arm also, and say that it is the Lord's will. Everything that comes to him is from the Lord. He does not show himself to men, and yet he is a magazine of love and of true and sweet ideas.

Next in order come the men with more Rajas, or activity, combative natures, who take up the ideas of the perfect ones and preach them to the world. The highest kind of men silently collect true and noble ideas, and others — the Buddhas and Christs — go from place to place preaching them and working for them. In the life of Gautama Buddha we notice him constantly saying that he is the twenty-fifth Buddha.

The twenty-four before him are unknown to history, although the Buddha known to history must have built upon foundations laid by them. The highest men are calm, silent, and unknown. They are the men who really know the power of thought; they are sure that, even if they go into a cave and close the door and simply think five true thoughts and then pass away, these five thoughts of theirs will live through eternity. Indeed such thoughts will penetrate through the mountains, cross the oceans, and travel through the world. They will enter deep into human hearts and brains and raise up men and women who will give them practical expression in the workings of human life. These Sattvika men are too near the Lord to be active and to fight, to be working, struggling, preaching and doing good, as they say, here on earth to humanity. The active workers, however good, have still a little remnant of ignorance left in them. When our nature has yet some impurities left in it, then alone can we work. It is in the nature of work to be impelled ordinarily by motive and by attachment. In the presence of an ever active Providence who notes even the sparrow's fall, how can man attach any importance to his own work? Will it not be a blasphemy to do so when we know that He is taking care of the minutest things in the world? We have only to stand in awe and reverence before Him saying, "Thy will be done". The highest men cannot work, for in them there is no attachment. Those whose whole soul is gone into the Self, those whose desires are confined in the Self, who have become ever associated with the Self, for them there is no work. Such are indeed the highest of mankind; but apart from them every one else has to work. In so working we should never think that we can help on even the least thing in this universe. We cannot. We only help ourselves in this gymnasium of the world. This is the proper attitude of work. If we work in this way, if we always remember that our present opportunity to work thus is a privilege which has been given to us, we shall never be attached to anything. Millions like you and me think that we are great people in the world; but we all die, and in five minutes the world forgets us. But the life of God is infinite. "Who can live a moment, breathe a moment, if this all-powerful One does not will it?" He is the ever active Providence. All power is His and within His command. Through His command the winds blow, the sun shines, the earth lives, and death stalks upon the earth. He is the all in all; He is all and in all. We can only worship Him. Give up all fruits of work; do good for its own sake; then alone will come perfect non-attachment. The bonds of the heart will thus break, and we shall reap perfect freedom. This freedom is indeed the goal of Karma-Yoga.

CHAPTER VIII
The Ideal of Karma-Yoga

The grandest idea in the religion of the Vedanta is that we may reach the same goal by different paths; and these paths I have generalised into four, viz those of work, love, psychology, and knowledge. But you must, at the same time, remember that these divisions are not very marked and quite exclusive of each other. Each blends into the other. But according to the type which prevails, we name the divisions. It is not that you can find men who have no other faculty than that of work, nor that you can find men who are no more than devoted worshippers only, nor that there are men who have no more than mere knowledge. These divisions are made in accordance with the type or the tendency that may be seen to prevail in a man. We have found that, in the end, all these four paths converge and become one. All religions and all methods of work and worship lead us to one and the same goal.

I have already tried to point out that goal. It is freedom as I understand it. Everything that we perceive around us is struggling towards freedom, from the atom to the man, from the insentient, lifeless particle of matter to the highest existence on earth, the human soul. The whole universe is in fact the result of this struggle for freedom. In all combinations every particle is trying to go on its own way, to fly from the other particles; but the others are holding it in check. Our earth is trying to fly away from the sun, and the moon from the earth. Everything has a tendency to infinite dispersion. All that we see in the universe has for its basis this one struggle towards freedom; it is under the impulse of this tendency that the saint prays and the robber robs. When the line of action taken is not a proper one, we call it evil; and when the manifestation of it is proper and high, we call it good. But the impulse is the same, the struggle towards freedom. The saint is oppressed with the knowledge of his condition of bondage, and he wants to get rid of it; so he worships God. The thief is oppressed with the idea that he does not possess certain things, and he tries to get rid of that want, to obtain freedom from it; so he steals. Freedom is the one goal of all nature, sentient or insentient; and consciously or unconsciously, everything is struggling towards that goal. The freedom which the saint seeks is very different from that which the robber seeks; the freedom loved by the saint leads him to the enjoyment of infinite, unspeakable bliss, while that on which the robber has set his heart only forges other bonds for his soul.

There is to be found in every religion the manifestation of this struggle towards freedom. It is the groundwork of all morality, of unselfishness, which means getting rid of the idea that men are the same as their little body. When we see a man doing good work, helping others, it means that he cannot be confined within the limited circle of "me and mine". There is no limit to this getting out of selfishness. All the great systems of ethics preach absolute unselfishness as the goal. Supposing this absolute unselfishness can be reached by a man, what becomes of him? He is no more the little Mr. So-and-so; he has acquired infinite expansion. The little personality which he had before is now lost to him for ever; he has become infinite, and the attainment of this infinite expansion is indeed the goal of all religions and of all moral and philosophical teachings. The personalist, when he hears this idea philosophically put, gets frightened. At the same time, if he preaches morality, he after all teaches the very same idea himself. He puts no limit to the unselfishness of man. Suppose a man becomes perfectly unselfish under the personalistic system, how are we to distinguish him from the perfected ones in other system? He has become one with the universe and to become that is the goal of all; only the poor personalist has not the courage to follow out his own reasoning to its right conclusion. Karma-Yoga is the attaining through unselfish work of that freedom which is the goal of all human nature. Every selfish action, therefore, retards our reaching the goal, and every unselfish action takes us towards the goal; that is why the only definition that can be given of morality is this: *That which is selfish is immoral, and that which is unselfish is moral.*

But, if you come to details, the matter will not be seen to be quite so simple. For instance, environment often makes the details different as I have already mentioned. The same action under one set of circumstances may be unselfish, and under another set quite selfish. So we can give only a general definition, and leave the details to be worked out by taking into consideration the differences in time, place, and circumstances. In one country one kind of conduct is considered moral, and in another the very same is immoral, because the circumstances differ. The goal of all nature is freedom, and freedom is to be attained only by perfect unselfishness; every thought, word, or deed that is unselfish takes us towards the goal, and, as such, is called moral. That definition, you will find, holds good in every religion and every system of ethics. In some systems of thought morality is derived from a Superior Being — God. If you ask why a man ought to do this and not that, their answer is: "Because such is the command of God." But whatever be the source from which it is derived, their code of ethics also has the same central idea — not to think of self but to give up self. And yet some persons, in spite of this high ethical idea, are frightened at the thought of having to give up their little personalities. We may ask the man who clings to the idea of little personalities to consider the case of a person who has become perfectly unselfish, who has no thought for himself, who does no deed for himself, who speaks no word for himself, and then say where his "himself" is. That "himself" is known to him only so long as he thinks, acts, or speaks for himself. If he is only conscious of others, of the universe, and of the all, where is his "himself"? It is gone for ever.

Karma-Yoga, therefore, is a system of ethics and religion intended to attain freedom through unselfishness, and by good works. The Karma-Yogi need not believe in any doctrine whatever. He may not believe even in God, may not ask what his soul is, nor think of any metaphysical speculation. He has got his own special aim of realising selflessness; and he has to work it out himself. Every moment of his life must be realisation, because he has to solve by mere work, without the help of doctrine or theory, the very same problem to which the Jnâni applies his reason and inspiration and the Bhakta his love.

Now comes the next question: What is this work? What is this doing good to the world? Can we do good to the world? In an absolute sense, no; in a relative sense, yes. No permanent or everlasting good can be done to the world; if it could be done, the world would not be this world. We may satisfy the hunger of a man for five minutes, but he will be hungry again. Every pleasure with which we supply a man may be seen to be momentary. No one can permanently cure this ever-recurring fever of pleasure and pain. Can any permanent happiness be given to the world? In the ocean we cannot raise a wave without causing a hollow somewhere else. The sum total of the good things in the world has been the same throughout in its relation to man's need and greed. It cannot be increased or decreased. Take the history of the human race as we know it today. Do we not find the same miseries and the same happiness, the same pleasures and pains, the same differences in position? Are not some rich, some poor, some high, some low, some healthy, some unhealthy? All this was just the same with the Egyptians, the Greeks, and the Romans in ancient times as it is with the Americans today. So far as history is known, it has always been the same; yet at the same time we find that, running along with all these incurable differences of pleasure and pain, there has ever been the struggle to alleviate them. Every period of history has given birth to thousands of men and women who have worked hard to smooth the passage of life for others. And how far have they succeeded? We can only play at driving the ball from one place to another. We take away pain from the physical plane, and it goes to the mental one. It is like that picture in Dante's hell where the misers were given a mass of gold to roll up a hill. Every time they rolled it up a little, it again rolled down. All our talks about the millennium are very nice as school-boys' stories, but they are no better than that. All nations that dream of the millennium also think that, of all peoples in the world, they will have the best of it then for themselves. This is the wonderfully unselfish idea of the millennium!

We cannot add happiness to this world; similarly, we cannot add pain to it either. The sum total of the energies of pleasure and pain displayed here on earth will be the same throughout. We just push it from this side to the other side, and from that side to this, but it will remain the same, because to remain so is its very nature. This ebb and flow, this rising and falling, is in the world's very nature; it would be as logical to hold otherwise as to say that we may have life without death. This is complete nonsense, because the very idea of life implies death and the very idea of pleasure implies pain. The lamp is constantly burning out, and that is its life. If you want to have life, you have to die every moment for it. Life and death are only different expressions of the same thing looked at from different standpoints; they are the falling and the rising of the same wave, and the two form one whole. One looks at the "fall" side and becomes a pessimist another looks at the "rise" side and becomes an optimist. When a boy is going to school and his father and mother are taking care of him, everything seems blessed to him; his wants are simple, he is a great optimist. But the old man, with his varied experience, becomes calmer and is sure to have his warmth considerably cooled down. So, old nations, with signs of decay all around them, are apt to be less hopeful than new nations. There is a proverb in India: "A thousand years a city, and a thousand years a forest." This change of city into forest and vice versa is going on everywhere, and it makes people optimists or pessimists according to the side they see of it.

The next idea we take up is the idea of equality. These millennium ideas have been great motive powers to work. Many religions preach this as an element in them — that God is coming to rule the universe, and that then there will be no difference at all in conditions. The people who preach this doctrine are mere fanatics, and fanatics are indeed the sincerest of mankind. Christianity was preached just on the basis of the fascination of this fanaticism, and that is what made it so attractive to the Greek and the Roman slaves. They believed that under the millennial religion there would be no more slavery, that there would be plenty to eat and drink; and, therefore, they flocked round the Christian standard. Those who preached the idea first were of course ignorant fanatics, but very sincere. In modern times this millennial aspiration takes the form of equality — of liberty, equality, and fraternity. This is also fanaticism. True equality has never been and never can be on earth. How can we all be equal here? This impossible kind of equality implies total death. What makes this world what it is? Lost balance. In the primal state, which is called chaos, there is perfect balance. How do all the formative forces of the universe come then? By struggling, competition, conflict. Suppose that all the particles of matter were held in equilibrium, would there be then any process of creation? We know from science that it is impossible. Disturb a sheet of water, and there you find every particle of the water trying to become calm again, one rushing against the other; and in the same way all the phenomena which we call the universe — all things therein — are struggling to get back to the state of perfect balance. Again a disturbance comes, and again we have combination and creation. Inequality is the very basis of creation. At the same time the forces struggling to obtain equality are as much a necessity of creation as those which destroy it.

Absolute equality, that which means a perfect balance of all the struggling forces in all the planes, can never be in this world. Before you attain that state, the world will have become quite unfit for any kind of life, and no one will be there. We find, therefore, that all these ideas of the millennium and of absolute equality are not only impossible but also that, if we try to carry them out, they will lead us surely enough to the day of destruction. What makes the difference between man and man? It is largely the difference in the brain. Nowadays no one but a lunatic will say that we are all born with the same brain power. We come into the world with unequal endowments; we come as greater men or as lesser men, and there is no getting away from that pre-natally determined condition. The

American Indians were in this country for thousands of years, and a few handfuls of your ancestors came to their land. What difference they have caused in the appearance of the country! Why did not the Indians make improvements and build cities, if all were equal? With your ancestors a different sort of brain power came into the land, different bundles of past impressions came, and they worked out and manifested themselves. Absolute non-differentiation is death. So long as this world lasts, differentiation there will and must be, and the millennium of perfect equality will come only when a cycle of creation comes to its end. Before that, equality cannot be. Yet this idea of realising the millennium is a great motive power. Just as inequality is necessary for creation itself, so the struggle to limit it is also necessary. If there were no struggle to become free and get back to God, there would be no creation either. It is the difference between these two forces that determines the nature of the motives of men. There will always be these motives to work, some tending towards bondage and others towards freedom.

This world's wheel within wheel is a terrible mechanism; if we put our hands in it, as soon as we are caught we are gone. We all think that when we have done a certain duty, we shall be at rest; but before we have done a part of that duty, another is already in waiting. We are all being dragged along by this mighty, complex world-machine. There are only two ways out of it; one is to give up all concerns with the machine, to let it go and stand aside, to give up our desires. That is very easy to say, but is almost impossible to do. I do not know whether in twenty millions of men one can do that. The other way is to plunge into the world and learn the secret of work, and that is the way of Karma-Yoga. Do not fly away from the wheels of the world-machine, but stand inside it and learn the secret of work. Through proper work done inside, it is also possible to come out. Through this machinery itself is the way out.

We have now seen what work is. It is a part of natures foundation, and goes on always. Those that believe in God understand this better, because they know that God is not such an incapable being as will need our help. Although this universe will go on always, our goal is freedom, our goal is unselfishness; and according to Karma-Yoga, that goal is to be reached through work. All ideas of making the world perfectly happy may be good as motive powers for fanatics; but we must know that fanaticism brings forth as much evil as good. The Karma-Yogi asks why you require any motive to work other than the inborn love of freedom. Be beyond the common worldly motives. "To work you have the right, but not to the fruits thereof." Man can train himself to know and to practice that, says the Karma-Yogi. When the idea of doing good becomes a part of his very being, then he will not seek for any motive outside. Let us do good because it is good to do good; he who does good work even in order to get to heaven binds himself down, says the Karma-Yogi. Any work that is done with any the least selfish motive, instead of making us free, forges one more chain for our feet.

So the only way is to give up all the fruits of work, to be unattached to them. Know that this world is not we, nor are we this world; that we are really not the body; that we really do not work. We are the Self, eternally at rest and at peace. Why should we be bound by anything? It is very good to say that we should be perfectly non-attached, but what is the way to do it? Every good work we do without any ulterior motive, instead of forging a new chain, will break one of the links in the existing chains. Every good thought that we send to the world without thinking of any return, will be stored up there and break one link in the chain, and make us purer and purer, until we become the purest of mortals. Yet all this may seem to be rather quixotic and too philosophical, more theoretical than practical. I have read many arguments against the Bhagavad-Gita, and many have said that without motives you cannot work. They have never seen unselfish work except under the influence of fanaticism, and, therefore, they speak in that way.

Let me tell you in conclusion a few words about one man who actually carried this teaching of Karma-Yoga into practice. That man is Buddha. He is the one man who ever carried this into perfect practice. All the prophets of the world, except Buddha, had external motives to move them to unselfish action. The prophets of the world, with this single exception, may be divided into two sets, one set holding that they are incarnations of God come down on earth, and the other holding that they are only messengers from God; and both draw their impetus for work from outside, expect reward from outside, however highly spiritual may be the language they use. But Buddha is the only prophet who said, "I do not care to know your various theories about God. What is the use of discussing all the subtle doctrines about the soul? Do good and be good. And this will take you to freedom and to whatever truth there is." He was, in the conduct of his life, absolutely without personal motives; and what man worked more than he? Show me in history one character who has soared so high above all. The whole human race has produced but one such character, such high philosophy, such wide sympathy. This great philosopher, preaching the highest philosophy, yet had the deepest sympathy for the lowest of animals, and never put forth any claims for himself. He is the ideal Karma-Yogi, acting entirely without motive, and the history of humanity shows him to have been the greatest man ever born; beyond compare the greatest combination of heart and brain that ever existed, the greatest soul-power that has even been manifested. He is the first great reformer the world has seen. He was the first who dared to say, "Believe not because some old manuscripts are produced, believe not because it is your national belief, because you have been made to believe it from your childhood; but reason it all out, and after you have analysed it, then, if you find that it will do Wgood to one and all, believe it, live up to it, and help others to live up to it." He works best who works without any motive, neither for money, nor for fame, nor for anything else; and when a man can do that, he will be a Buddha, and out of him will come the power to work in such a manner as will transform the world. This man represents the very highest ideal of Karma-Yoga.

Prem-Yoga

CHAPTER I
The Preparatory Renunciation

We have now finished the consideration of what may be called the preparatory Bhakti, and are entering on the study of the Parâ-Bhakti or supreme devotion. We have to speak of a preparation to the practice of this Para-Bhakti. All such preparations are intended only for the purification of the soul. The repetition of names, the rituals, the forms, and the symbols, all these various things are for the purification of the soul. The greatest purifier among all such things, a purifier without which no one can enter the regions of this higher devotion (Para-Bhakti), is renunciation. This frightens many; yet, without it, there cannot be any spiritual growth. In all our Yogas this renunciation is necessary. This is the stepping-stone and the real centre and the real heart of all spiritual culture — renunciation. This is religion — renunciation.

When the human soul draws back from the things of the world and tries to go into deeper things; when man, the spirit which has here somehow become concretised and materialised, understands that he is thereby going to be destroyed and to be reduced almost into mere matter, and turns his face away from matter — then begins renunciation, then begins real spiritual growth. The Karma-Yogi's renunciation is in the shape of giving up all the fruits of his action; he is not attached to the results of his labour; he does not care for any reward here or hereafter. The Râja-Yogi knows that the whole of nature is intended for the soul to acquire experience, and that the result of all the experiences of the soul is for it to become aware of its eternal separateness from nature. The human soul has to understand and realise that it has been spirit, and not matter, through eternity, and that this conjunction of it with matter is and can be only for a time. The Raja-Yogi learns the lesson of renunciation through his own experience of nature. The Jnâna-Yogi has the harshest of all renunciations to go through, as he has to realise from the very first that the whole of this solid-looking nature is all an illusion. He has to understand that all that is any kind of manifestation of power in nature belongs to the soul, and not to nature. He has to know from the very start that all knowledge and all experience are in the soul and not in nature; so he has at once and by the sheer force of rational conviction to tear himself away from all bondage to nature. He lets nature and all that belongs to her go, he lets them vanish and tries to stand alone!

Of all renunciations, the most natural, so to say, is that of the Bhakti-Yogi. Here there is no violence, nothing to give up, nothing to tear off, as it were, from ourselves, nothing from which we have violently to separate ourselves. The Bhakta's renunciation is easy, smooth flowing, and as natural as the things around us. We see the manifestation of this sort of renunciation, although more or less in the form of caricatures, every day around us. A man begins to love a woman; after a while he loves another, and the first woman he lets go. She drops out of his mind smoothly, gently, without his feeling the want of her at all. A woman loves a man; she then begins to love another man, and the first one drops off from her mind quite naturally. A man loves his own city, then he begins to love his country, and the intense love for his little city drops off smoothly, naturally. Again, a man learns to love the whole world; his love for his country, his intense, fanatical patriotism drops off without hurting him, without any manifestation of violence. An uncultured man loves the pleasures of the senses intensely; as he becomes cultured, he begins to love intellectual pleasures, and his sense-enjoyments become less and less. No man can enjoy a meal with the same gusto or pleasure as a dog or a wolf, but those pleasures which a man gets from intellectual experiences and achievements, the dog can never enjoy. At first, pleasure is in association with the lowest senses; but as soon as an animal reaches a higher plane of existence, the lower kind of pleasures becomes less intense. In human society, the nearer the man is to the animal, the stronger is his pleasure in the senses; and the higher and the more cultured the man is, the greater is his pleasure in intellectual and such other finer pursuits. So when a man gets even higher than the plane of the intellect, higher than that of mere thought, when he gets to the plane of spirituality and of divine inspiration, he finds there a state of bliss, compared with which all the pleasures of the senses, or even of the intellect, are as nothing. When the moon shines brightly, all the stars become dim; and when the sun shines, the moon herself becomes dim. The renunciation necessary for the attainment of Bhakti is not obtained by killing anything, but just comes in as naturally as in the presence of an increasingly stronger light, the less intense ones become dimmer and dimmer until they vanish away completely. So this love of the pleasures of the senses and of the intellect is all made dim and thrown aside and cast into the shade by the love of God Himself.

That love of God grows and assumes a form which is called Para-Bhakti or supreme devotion. Forms vanish, rituals fly away, books are superseded; images, temples, churches, religions and sects, countries and nationalities — all these little limitations and bondages fall off by their own nature from him who knows this love of God. Nothing remains to bind him or fetter his freedom. A ship, all of a sudden, comes near a magnetic rock, and its iron bolts and bars are all attracted and drawn out, and the planks get loosened and freely float on the water. Divine grace thus loosens the binding bolts and bars of the soul, and it becomes free. So in this renunciation auxiliary to devotion, there is no harshness, no dryness no struggle, nor repression nor suppression. The Bhakta has not to suppress any single one of his emotions, he only strives to intensify them and direct them to God.

CHAPTER II
The Bhakta's Renunciation Results From Love

We see love everywhere in nature. Whatever in society is good and great and sublime is the working out of that love; whatever in society is very bad, nay diabolical, is also the ill-directed working out of the same emotion of love. It is this same emotion that gives us the pure and holy conjugal love between husband and wife as well as the sort of love which goes to satisfy the lowest forms of animal passion. The emotion is the same, but its manifestation is different in different cases. It is the same feeling of love, well or ill directed, that impels one man to do good and to give all he has to the poor, while it makes another man cut the throats of his brethren and take away all their possessions. The former loves others as much as the latter loves himself. The direction of the love is bad in the case of the latter, but it is right and proper in the other case. The same fire that cooks a meal for us may burn a child, and it is no fault of the fire if it does so; the difference lies in the way in which it is used. Therefore love, the intense longing for association, the strong desire on the part of two to become one — and it may be, after all, of all to become merged in one — is being manifested everywhere in higher or lower forms as the case may be.

Bhakti-Yoga is the science of higher love. It shows us how to direct it; it shows us how to control it, how to manage it, how to use it, how to give it a new aim, as it were, and from it obtain the highest and most glorious results, that is, how to make it lead us to spiritual blessedness. Bhakti-Yoga does not say, "Give up"; it only says, "Love; love the Highest!" — and everything low naturally falls off from him, the object of whose love is the Highest.

"I cannot tell anything about Thee except that Thou art my love. Thou art beautiful, Oh, Thou art beautiful! Thou art beauty itself." What is after all really required of us in this Yoga is that our thirst after the beautiful should be directed to God. What is the beauty in the human face, in the sky, in the stars, and in the moon? It is only the partial apprehension of the real all-embracing Divine Beauty. "He shining, everything shines. It is through His light that all things shine." Take this high position of Bhakti which makes you forget at once all your little personalities. Take yourself away from all the world's little selfish clingings. Do not look upon humanity as the centre of all your human and higher interests. Stand as a witness, as a student, and observe the phenomena of nature. Have the feeling of personal non-attachment with regard to man, and see how this mighty feeling of love is working itself out in the world. Sometimes a little friction is produced, but that is only in the course of the struggle to attain the higher real love. Sometimes there is a little fight or a little fall; but it is all only by the way. Stand aside, and freely let these frictions come. You feel the frictions only when you are in the current of the world, but when you are outside of it simply as a witness and as a student, you will be able to see that there are millions and millions of channels in which God is manifesting Himself as Love.

"Wherever there is any bliss, even though in the most sensual of things, there is a spark of that Eternal Bliss which is the Lord Himself." Even in the lowest kinds of attraction there is the germ of divine love. One of the names of the Lord in Sanskrit is Hari, and this means that He attracts all things to Himself. His is in fact the only attraction worthy of human hearts. Who can attract a soul really? Only He! Do you think dead matter can truly attract the soul? It never did, and never will. When you see a man going after a beautiful face, do you think that it is the handful of arranged material molecules which really attracts the man? Not at all. Behind those material particles there must be and is the play of divine influence and divine love. The ignorant man does not know it, but yet, consciously or unconsciously, he is attracted by it and it alone. So even the lowest forms of attraction derive their power from God Himself. "None, O beloved, ever loved the husband for the husband's sake; it is the Âtman, the Lord who is within, for whose sake the husband is loved." Loving wives may know this or they may not; it is true all the same. "None, O beloved, ever loved the wife for the wife's sake, but it is the Self in the wife that is loved." Similarly, no one loves a child or anything else in the world except on account of Him who is within. The Lord is the great magnet, and we are all like iron filings; we are being constantly attracted by Him, and all of us are struggling to reach Him. All this struggling of ours in this world is surely not intended for selfish ends. Fools do not know what they are doing: the work of their life is, after all, to approach the great magnet. All the tremendous struggling and fighting in life is intended to make us go to Him ultimately and be one with Him.

The Bhakti-Yogi, however, knows the meaning of life's struggles; he understands it. He has passed through a long series of these struggles and knows what they mean and earnestly desires to be free from the friction thereof; he wants to avoid the clash and go direct to the centre of all attraction, the great Hari This is the renunciation of the Bhakta. This mighty attraction in the direction of God makes all other attractions vanish for him. This mighty infinite love of God which enters his heart leaves no place for any other love to live there. How can it be otherwise" Bhakti fills his heart with the divine waters of the ocean of love, which is God Himself; there is no place there for little loves. That is to say, the Bhakta's renunciation is that Vairâgya or non-attachment for all things that are not God which results from Anurâga or great attachment to God.

This is the ideal preparation for the attainment of the supreme Bhakti. When this renunciation comes, the gate opens for the soul to pass through and reach the lofty regions of supreme devotion or Para-Bhakti. Then it is that we begin to understand what Para-Bhakti is; and the man who has entered into the inner shrine of the Para-Bhakti alone has the right to say that all forms and symbols are useless to him as aids to religious realisation. He alone has attained that supreme state of love commonly called the brotherhood of man; the rest only talk. He sees no distinctions; the mighty ocean of love has entered into him, and he sees not man in man, but beholds his Beloved everywhere. Through every face shines to him his Hari. The light in the sun or the moon is all His manifestation. Wherever there is beauty or sublimity, to him it is all His. Such Bhaktas are still living; the world is never without them. Such, though bitten by a serpent, only say that a messenger came to them from their Beloved. Such men alone have the right to talk of universal brotherhood. They feel no resentment; their minds never react in the form of hatred or jealousy. The external, the sensuous, has vanished from them for ever. How can they be angry, when, through their love, they are always able to see the Reality behind the scenes?

CHAPTER III
The Naturalness of Bhakti-Yoga and Its Central Secret

"Those who with constant attention always worship You, and those who worship the Undifferentiated, the Absolute, of these who are the greatest Yogis?" — Arjuna asked of Shri Krishna. The answer was: "Those who concentrating their minds on Me worship Me with eternal constancy and are endowed with the highest faith, they are My best worshippers, they are the greatest Yogis. Those that worship the Absolute, the Indescribable, the Undifferentiated, the Omnipresent, the Unthinkable, the All-comprehending, the Immovable, and the Eternal, by controlling the play of their organs and having the conviction of sameness in regard to all things, they also, being engaged in doing good to all beings, come to Me alone. But to those whose minds have been devoted to the unmanifested Absolute, the difficulty of the struggle along the way is much greater, for it is indeed with great difficulty that the path of the unmanifested Absolute is trodden by any embodied being. Those who, having offered up all their work unto Me, with entire reliance on Me, meditate on Me and worship Me without any attachment to anything else — them, I soon lift up from the ocean of ever-recurring births and deaths, as their mind is wholly attached to Me" (Gita, XII).

Jnâna-Yoga and Bhakti-Yoga are both referred to here. Both may be said to have been defined in the above passage. Jnana-Yoga is grand; it is high philosophy; and almost every human being thinks, curiously enough, that he can surely do everything required of him by philosophy; but it is really very difficult to live truly the life of philosophy. We are often apt to run into great dangers in trying to guide our life by philosophy. This world may be said to be divided between persons of demoniacal nature who think the care-taking of the body to be the be-all and the end-all of existence, and persons of godly nature who realise that the body is simply a means to an end, an instrument intended for the culture of the soul. The devil can and indeed does cite the scriptures for his own purpose; and thus the way of knowledge appears to offer justification to what the bad man does, as much as it offers inducements to what the good man does. This is the great danger in Jnana-Yoga. But Bhakti-Yoga is natural, sweet, and gentle; the Bhakta does not take such high flights as the Jnana-Yogi, and, therefore, he is not apt to have such big falls. Until the bondages of the soul pass away, it cannot of course be free, whatever may be the nature of the path that the religious man takes.

Here is a passage showing how, in the case of one of the blessed Gopis, the soul-binding chains of both merit and demerit were broken. "The intense pleasure in meditating on God took away the binding effects of her good deeds. Then her intense misery of soul in not attaining unto Him washed off all her sinful propensities; and then she became free." —

तच्चिन्ताविपुलाह्लादक्षीणपुण्यचया तथा। तदप्राप्ति महदुःखविलीनाशेषपातका॥
निरुच्छ्वासतया मुक्तिं गतान्या गोपकन्यका॥

(Vishnu-Purâna). In Bhakti-Yoga the central secret is, therefore, to know that the various passions and feelings and emotions in the human heart are not wrong in themselves; only they have to be carefully controlled and given a higher and higher direction, until they attain the very highest condition of excellence. The highest direction is that which takes us to God; every other direction is lower. We find that pleasures and pains are very common and oft-recurring feelings in our lives. When a man feels pain because he has not wealth or some such worldly thing, he is giving a wrong direction to the feeling. Still pain has its uses. Let a man feel pain that he has not reached the Highest, that he has not reached God, and that pain will be to his salvation. When you become glad that you have a handful of coins, it is a wrong direction given to the faculty of joy;

it should be given a higher direction, it must be made to serve the Highest Ideal. Pleasure in that kind of ideal must surely be our highest joy. This same thing is true of all our other feelings. The Bhakta says that not one of them is wrong, he gets hold of them all and points them unfailingly towards God.

CHAPTER IV
The Forms of Love — Manifestation

Here are some of the forms in which love manifests itself. First there is reverence. Why do people show reverence to temples and holy places? Because He is worshipped there, and His presence is associated with all such places. Why do people in every country pay reverence to teachers of religion? It is natural for the human heart to do so, because all such teachers preach the Lord. At bottom, reverence is a growth out of love; we can none of us revere him whom we do not love. Then comes Priti — pleasure in God. What an immense pleasure men take in the objects of the senses. They go anywhere, run through any danger, to get the thing which they love, the thing which their senses like. What is wanted of the Bhakta is this very kind of intense love which has, however, to be directed to God. Then there is the sweetest of pains, Viraha, the intense misery due to the absence of the beloved. When a man feels intense misery because he has not attained to God, has not known that which is the only thing worthy to be known, and becomes in consequence very dissatisfied and almost mad — then there is Viraha; and this state of the mind makes him feel disturbed in the presence of anything other than the beloved (Ekarativichikitsâ). In earthly love we see how often this Viraha comes. Again, when men are really and intensely in love with women or women with men, they feel a kind of natural annoyance in the presence of all those whom they do not love. Exactly the same state of impatience in regard to things that are not loved comes to the mind when Para-Bhakti holds sway over it; even to talk about things other than God becomes distasteful then. "Think of Him, think of Him alone, and give up all other vain words" अन्या वाचो विमुंचथ। — Those who talk of Him alone, the Bhakta finds to be friendly to him; while those who talk of anything else appear to him to be unfriendly. A still higher stage of love is reached when life itself is maintained for the sake of the one Ideal of Love, when life itself is considered beautiful and worth living only on account of that Love (तदर्थप्राणसंस्थानं). Without it, such a life would not remain even for a moment. Life is sweet, because it thinks of the Beloved. Tadiyatâ (*His-ness*) comes when a man becomes perfect according to Bhakti — when he has become blessed, when he has attained God, when he has touched the feet of God, as it were. Then his whole nature is purified and completely changed. All his purpose in life then becomes fulfilled. Yet many such Bhaktas live on just to worship Him. That is the bliss, the only pleasure in life which they will not give up. "O king, such is the blessed quality of Hari that even those who have become satisfied with everything, all the knots of whose hearts have been cut asunder, even they love the Lord for love's sake" — the Lord "Whom all the gods worship — all the lovers of liberation, and all the knowers of the Brahman" — यं सर्वे देवा नमन्ति मुमुक्षवो ब्रह्मवादिनश्चेति (*Nri. Tap. Up.*). Such is the power of love. When a man has forgotten himself altogether, and does not feel that anything belongs to him, then he acquires the state of Tadiyata; everything is sacred to him, because it belongs to the Beloved. Even in regard to earthly love, the lover thinks that everything belonging to his beloved is sacred and so dear to him. He loves even a piece of cloth belonging to the darling of his heart In the same way, when a person loves the Lord, the whole universe becomes dear to him, because it is all His.

CHAPTER V
Universal Love and How it Leads to Self-Surrender

How can we love the Vyashti, the particular, without first loving the Samashti, the universal? God is the Samashti, the generalised and the abstract universal whole; and the universe that we see is the Vyashti, the particularised thing. To love the whole universe is possible only by way of loving the Samashti — the universal — which is, as it were, the one unity in which are to be found millions and millions of smaller unities. The philosophers of India do not stop at the particulars; they cast a hurried glance at the particulars and immediately start to find the generalised forms which will include all the particulars. The search after the universal is the one search of Indian philosophy and religion. The Jnâni aims at the wholeness of things, at that one absolute and; generalised Being, knowing which he knows everything. The Bhakta wishes to realise that one generalised abstract Person, in loving whom he loves the whole universe. The Yogi wishes to have possession of that one generalised form of power, by controlling which he controls this whole universe. The Indian mind, throughout its history, has been directed to this kind of singular search after the universal in everything — in science, in psychology, in love, in philosophy. So the conclusion to which the Bhakta comes is that, if you go on merely loving one, person after another, you may go on loving them so for an infinite length of time, without being in the least able to love the world as a whole. When, at last, the central idea is, however, arrived at that the sum total of all love is God, that the sum total of the aspirations of all the souls in the universe, whether they be free, or bound, or struggling towards liberation, is God, then alone it becomes possible for any one to put forth universal love. God is the Samashti, and this visible universe is God differentiated and made manifest. If we love this sum total, we love everything. Loving the world doing it good will all come easily then; we have to obtain this power only by loving God first; otherwise it is no joke to do good to the world. "Everything is His and He is my Lover; I love Him," says the Bhakta. In this way everything becomes sacred to the Bhakta, because all things are His. All are His children, His body, His manifestation. How then may we hurt any one? How then may we not love any one? With the love of God will come, as a sure effect, the love of every one in the universe. The nearer we approach God, the more do we begin to see that all things are in Him. When the soul succeeds in appropriating the bliss of this supreme love, it also begins to see Him in everything. Our heart will thus become an eternal fountain of love. And when we reach even higher states of this love, all the little differences between the things of the world are entirely lost; man is seen no more as man, but only as God; the animal is seen no more as animal, but as God; even the tiger is no more a tiger, but a manifestation of God. Thus in this intense state of Bhakti, worship is offered to every one, to every life, and to every being. एवं सर्वेषु भूतेषु भक्तिरव्यभिचारिणी । कर्तव्या पण्डितैर्ज्ञात्वा सर्वभूतमयं हरिम् ॥ — "Knowing that Hari, the Lord, is in every being, the wise have thus to manifest unswerving love towards all beings."

As a result of this kind of intense all-absorbing love, comes the feeling of perfect self-surrender, the conviction that nothing that happens is against us, Aprâtikulya. Then the loving soul is able to say, if pain comes, "Welcome pain." If misery comes, it will say, "Welcome misery, you are also from the Beloved." If a serpent comes, it will say, "Welcome serpent." If death comes, such a Bhakta will welcome it with a smile. "Blessed am I that they all come to me; they are all welcome." The Bhakta in this state of perfect resignation, arising out of intense love to God and to all that are His, ceases to distinguish between pleasure and pain in so far as they affect him. He does not know what it is to complain of pain or misery; and this kind of uncomplaining resignation to the will of

God, who is all love, is indeed a worthier acquisition than all the glory of grand and heroic performances.

To the vast majority of mankind, the body is everything; the body is all the universe to them; bodily enjoyment is their all in all. This demon of the worship of the body and of the things of the body has entered into us all. We may indulge in tall talk and take very high flights, but we are like vultures all the same; our mind is directed to the piece of carrion down below. Why should our body be saved, say, from the tiger? Why may we not give it over to the tiger? The tiger will thereby be pleased, and that is not altogether so very far from self-sacrifice and worship. Can you reach the realization of such an idea in which all sense of self is completely lost? It is a very dizzy height on the pinnacle of the religion of love, and few in this world have ever climbed up to it; but until a man reaches that highest point of ever-ready and ever-willing self-sacrifice, he cannot become a perfect Bhakta. We may all manage to maintain our bodies more or less satisfactorily and for longer or shorter intervals of time. Nevertheless, our bodies have to go; there is no permanence about them. Blessed are they whose bodies get destroyed in the service of others. "Wealth, and even life itself, the sage always holds ready for the service of others. In this world, there being one thing certain, viz death, it is far better that this body dies in a good cause than in a bad one." We may drag our life on for fifty years or a hundred years; but after that, what is it that happens? Everything that is the result of combination must get dissolved and die. There must and will come a time for it to be decomposed. Jesus and Buddha and Mohammed are all dead; all the great Prophets and Teachers of the world are dead.

"In this evanescent world, where everything is falling to pieces, we have to make the highest use of what time we have," says the Bhakta; and really the highest use of life is to hold it at the service of all beings. It is the horrible body-idea that breeds all the selfishness in the world, just this one delusion that we are wholly the body we own, and that we must by all possible means try our very best to preserve and to please it. If you know that you are positively other than your body, you have then none to fight with or struggle against; you are dead to all ideas of selfishness. So the Bhakta declares that we have to hold ourselves as if we are altogether dead to all the things of the world; and that is indeed self-surrender. Let things come as they may. This is the meaning of "Thy will be done" — not going about fighting and struggling and thinking all the while that God wills all our own weaknesses and worldly ambitions. It may be that good comes even out of our selfish struggles; that is, however, God's look-out. The perfected Bhakta's idea must be never to will and work for himself. "Lord, they build high temples in Your name; they make large gifts in Your name; I am poor; I have nothing; so I take this body of mine and place it at Your feet. Do not give me up, O Lord." Such is the prayer proceeding out of the depths of the Bhakta's heart. To him who has experienced it, this eternal sacrifice of the self unto the Beloved Lord is higher by far than all wealth and power, than even all soaring thoughts of renown and enjoyment. The peace of the Bhakta's calm resignation is a peace that passeth all understanding and is of incomparable value. His Apratikulya is a state of the mind in which it has no interests and naturally knows nothing that is opposed to it. In this state of sublime resignation everything in the shape of attachment goes away completely, except that one all-absorbing love to Him in whom all things live and move and have their being. This attachment of love to God is indeed one that does not bind the soul but effectively breaks all its bondages.

CHAPTER VI
The Higher Knowledge and the Higher Love are One to the True Lover

The Upanishads distinguish between a higher knowledge and a lower knowledge; and to the Bhakta there is really no difference between this higher knowledge and his higher love (Parâ-Bhakti). The Mundaka Upanishad says:

द्वे विद्ये वेदितव्ये इति ह स्म यद्ब्रह्मविदो वदन्ति। परा चैवापरा च॥
तत्रापरा ऋग्वेदो यजुर्वदः सामवेदोऽथर्ववेदः शिक्षा कल्पो व्याकरणं निरुक्तं छन्दो
ज्योतिषमिति। अथ परा यया तदक्षरमधिगम्यते॥

— "The knowers of the Brahman declare that there are two kinds of knowledge worthy to be known, namely, the Higher (Parâ) and the lower (Aparâ). Of these the lower (knowledge) consists of the Rig-Veda, the Yajur-Veda, the Sâma-Veda, the Atharva-Veda, the Shikshâ (or the science dealing with pronunciation and accent), the Kalpa (or the sacrificial liturgy), grammar, the Nirukta (or the science dealing with etymology and the meaning of words), prosody, and astronomy; and the higher (knowledge) is that by which that Unchangeable is known."

The higher knowledge is thus clearly shown to be the knowledge of the Brahman; and the *Devi-Bhâgavata* gives us the following definition of the higher love (Para-Bhakti): "As oil poured from one vessel to another falls in an unbroken line, so, when the mind in an unbroken stream thinks of the Lord, we have what is called Para-Bhakti or supreme love." This kind of undisturbed and ever-steady direction of the mind and the heart to the Lord with an inseparable attachment is indeed the highest manifestation of man's love to God. All other forms of Bhakti are only preparatory to the attainment of this highest form thereof, viz the Para-Bhakti which is also known as the love that comes after attachment (Râgânugâ). When this supreme love once comes into the heart of man, his mind will continuously think of God and remember nothing else. He will give no room in himself to thoughts other than those of God, and his soul will be unconquerably pure and will alone break all the bonds of mind and matter and become serenely free. He alone can worship the Lord in his own heart; to him forms, symbols, books, and doctrines are all unnecessary and are incapable of proving serviceable in any way. It is not easy to love the Lord thus. Ordinarily human love is seen to flourish only in places where it is returned; where love is not returned for love, cold indifference is the natural result. There are, however, rare instances in which we may notice love exhibiting itself even where there is no return of love. We may compare this kind of love, for purposes of illustration, to the love of the moth for the fire; the insect loves the fire, falls into it, and dies. It is indeed in the nature of this insect to love so. To love because it is the nature of love to love is undeniably the highest and the most unselfish manifestation of love that may be seen in the world. Such love, working itself out on the plane of spirituality, necessarily leads to the attainment of Para-Bhakti.

CHAPTER VII
The Triangle
of Love

We may represent love as a triangle, each of the angles of which corresponds to one of its inseparable characteristics. There can be no triangle without all its three angles; and there can be no true love without its three following characteristics. The first angle of our triangle of love is that love knows no bargaining. Wherever there is any seeking for something in return, there can, be no real love; it becomes a mere matter of shop-keeping. As long as there is in us any idea of deriving this or that favour from God in return for our respect and allegiance to Him, so long there can be no true love growing in our hearts. Those who worship God because they wish Him to bestow favours on them are sure not to worship Him if those favours are not forthcoming. The Bhakta loves the Lord because He is lovable, there is no other motive originating or directing this divine emotion of the true devotee.

We have heard it said that a great king once went into a forest and there met a sage. He talked with the sage a little and was very much pleased with his purity and wisdom. The king then wanted the sage to oblige him by receiving a present from him. The sage refused to do so, saying, "The fruits of the forest are enough food for me; the pure streams of water flowing down from the mountains give enough drink for me; the barks of the trees supply me with enough covering; and the caves of the mountains form my home. Why should I take any present from you or from anybody?" The king said, "Just to benefit me, sir, please take something from my hands and please come with me to the city and to my palace." After much persuasion, the sage at last consented to do as the king desired and went with him to his palace. Before offering the gift to the sage, the king repeated his prayers, saying, "Lord, give me more children; Lord, give me more wealth; Lord, give me more territory; Lord, keep my body in better health", and so on. Before the king finished saying his prayer, the sage had got up and walked away from the room quietly. At this the king became perplexed and began to follow him, crying aloud, "Sir, you are going away, you have not received my gifts." The sage turned round to him and said, "I do not beg of beggars. You are yourself nothing but a beggar, and how can you give me anything? I am no fool to think of taking anything from a beggar like you. Go away, do not follow me."

There is well brought out the distinction between mere beggars and the real lovers of God. Begging is not the language of love. To worship God even for the sake of salvation or any other rewards equally degenerate. Love knows no reward. Love is always for love's sake. The Bhakta loves because he cannot help loving. When you see a beautiful scenery and fall in love with it, you do not demand anything in the way of favour from the scenery, nor does the scenery demand anything from you. Yet the vision thereof brings you to a blissful state of the mind; it tones down all the friction in your soul, it makes you calm, almost raises you, for the time being, beyond your mortal nature and places you in a condition of quiet divine ecstasy. This nature of real love is the first angle of our triangle. Ask not anything in return for your love; let your position be always that of the giver; give your love unto God, but do not ask anything in return even from Him.

The second angle of the triangle of love is that love knows no fear. Those that love God through fear are the lowest of human beings, quite undeveloped as men. They worship God from fear of punishment. He is a great Being to them, with a whip in one hand and the sceptre in the other; if they do not obey Him, they are afraid they will be whipped. It is a degradation to worship God through fear of punishment; such worship is, if worship at all, the crudest form of the worship of love. So long as there is any fear in the heart, how can there be love also? Love conquers naturally all fear. Think of a young mother in the street and a dog barking at her; she is frightened and flies into nearest house. But suppose the next day she is in the street with her child, and a lion springs upon the child. Where will be her position now? Of course, in the very mouth of the lion, protecting her child. Love conquers all fear. Fear comes from the selfish idea of cutting one's self off from the universe. The smaller and the more selfish I make myself, the more is my fear. If a man thinks he is a little nothing, fear will surely come upon him. And the less you think of yourself as an insignificant person, the less fear there will be for you. So long as there is the least spark of fear in you there can be no love there. Love and fear are incompatible; God is never to be feared by those who love Him. The commandment, "Do not take the name of the Lord thy God in vain", the true lover of God laughs at. How can there be any blasphemy in the religion of love? The more you take the name of the Lord, the better for you, in whatever way you may do it. You are only repeating His name because you love Him.

The third angle of the love-triangle is that love knows no rival, for in it is always embodied the lover's highest ideal. True love never comes until the object of our love becomes to us our highest ideal. It may be that in many cases human love is misdirected and misplaced, but to the person who loves, the thing he loves is always his own highest idea. One may see his ideal in the vilest of beings, and another in the highest of beings; nevertheless, in every case it is the ideal alone that can be truly and intensely loved. The highest ideal of every man is called God. Ignorant or wise, saint or sinner, man or woman, educated or uneducated, cultivated or uncultivated, to every human being the highest ideal is God. The synthesis of all the highest ideals of beauty, of sublimity, and of power gives us the completest conception of the loving and lovable God.

These ideals exist in some shape or other in every mind naturally; they form a part and parcel of all our minds. All the active manifestations of human nature are struggles of those ideals to become realised in practical life. All the various movements that we see around us in society are caused by the various ideals in various souls trying to come out and become concretised; what is inside presses on to come outside. This perennially dominant influence of the ideal is the one force, the one motive power, that may be seen to be constantly working in the midst of mankind. It may be after hundreds of births, after struggling through thousands of years, that man finds that it is vain to try to make the inner ideal mould completely the external conditions and square well with them; after realising this he no more tries to project his own ideal on the outside world, but worships the ideal itself as ideal from the highest standpoint of love. This ideally perfect ideal embraces all lower ideals. Every one admits the truth of the saying that a lover sees Helen's beauty on an Ethiop's brow. The man who is standing aside as a looker-on sees that love is here misplaced, but the lover sees his Helen all the same and does not see the Ethiop at all. Helen or Ethiop, the objects of our love are really the centres round which our ideals become crystallised. What is it that the world commonly worships? Not certainly this all-embracing, ideally perfect ideal of the supreme devotee and lover. That ideal which men and women commonly worship is what is in themselves; every person projects his or her own ideal on the outside world and kneels before it. That is why we find that men who are cruel and blood-thirsty conceive of a bloodthirsty God, because they can only love their own highest ideal. That is why good men have a very high ideal of God, and their ideal is indeed so very different from that of others.

CHAPTER VIII
The God of Love is His Own Proof

What is the ideal of the lover who has quite passed beyond the idea of selfishness, of bartering and bargaining, and who knows no fear? Even to the great God such a man will say, "I will give You my all, and I do not want anything from You; indeed there is nothing that I can call my own." When a man has acquired this conviction, his ideal becomes one of perfect love, one of perfect fearlessness of love. The highest ideal of such a person has no narrowness of particularity about it; it is love universal, love without limits and bonds, love itself, absolute love. This grand ideal of the religion of love is worshipped and loved absolutely as such without the aid of any symbols or suggestions. This is the highest form of Para-Bhakti — the worship of such an all-comprehending ideal as the ideal; all the other forms of Bhakti are only stages on the way to reach it.

All our failures and all our successes in following the religion of love are on the road to the realisation of that one ideal. Object after object is taken up, and the inner ideal is successively projected on them all; and all such external objects are found inadequate as exponents of the ever-expanding inner ideal and are naturally rejected one after another. At last the aspirant begins to think that it is vain to try to realise the ideal in external objects, that all external objects are as nothing when compared with the ideal itself; and, in course of time, he acquires the power of realising the highest and the most generalised abstract ideal entirely as an abstraction that is to him quite alive and real. When the devotee has reached this point, he is no more impelled to ask whether God can be demonstrated or not, whether He is omnipotent and omniscient or not. To him He is only the God of Love; He is the highest ideal of love, and that is sufficient for all his purposes. He, as love, is self-evident. It requires no proofs to demonstrate the existence of the beloved to the lover. The magistrate-Gods of other forms of religion may require a good deal of proof prove Them, but the Bhakta does not and cannot think of such Gods at all. To him God exists entirely as love. "None, O beloved, loves the husband for the husband's sake, but it is for the sake of the Self who is in the husband that the husband is loved; none, O beloved, loves the wife for the wife's sake, but it is for the sake of the Self who is in the wife that the wife is loved."

It is said by some that selfishness is the only motive power in regard to all human activities. That also is love lowered by being particularised. When I think of myself as comprehending the Universal, there can surely be no selfishness in me; but when I, by mistake, think that I am a little something, my love becomes particularized and narrowed. The mistake consists in making the sphere of love narrow and contracted. All things in the universe are of divine origin and deserve to be loved; it has, however, to be borne in mind that the love of the whole includes the love of the parts. This whole is the God of the Bhaktas, and all the other Gods, Fathers in Heaven, or Rulers, or Creators, and all theories and doctrines and books have no purpose and no meaning for them, seeing that they have through their supreme love and devotion risen above those things altogether. When the heart is purified and cleansed and filled to the brim with the divine nectar of love, all other ideas of God become simply puerile and are rejected as being inadequate or unworthy. Such is indeed the power of Para-Bhakti or Supreme Love; and the perfected Bhakta no more goes to see God in temples and churches; he knows no place where he will not find Him. He finds Him in the temple as well as out of the temple, he finds Him in the saint's saintliness as well as in the wicked man's wickedness, because he has Him already seated in glory in his own heart as the one Almighty inextinguishable Light of Love which is ever shining and eternally present.

CHAPTER IX
Human Representations of the Divine Ideal of Love

It is impossible to express the nature of this supreme and absolute ideal of love in human language. Even the highest flight of human imagination is incapable of comprehending it in all its infinite perfection and beauty. Nevertheless, the followers of the religion of love, in its higher as well as its lower forms, in all countries, have all along had to use the inadequate human language to comprehend and to define their own ideal of love. Nay more, human love itself, in all its varied forms has been made to typify this inexpressible divine love. Man can think of divine things only in his own human way, to us the Absolute can be expressed only in our relative language. The whole universe is to us a writing of the Infinite in the language of the finite. Therefore Bhaktas make use of all the common terms associated with the common love of humanity in relation to God and His worship through love.

Some of the great writers on Para-Bhakti have tried to understand and experience this divine love in so many different ways. The lowest form in which this love is apprehended is what they call the peaceful — the Shânta. When a man worships God without the fire of love in him, without its madness in his brain, when his love is just the calm commonplace love, a little higher than mere forms and ceremonies and symbols, but not at all characterized by the madness of intensely active love, it is said to be Shanta. We see some people in the world who like to move on slowly, and others who come and go like the whirlwind. The Shânta-Bhakta is calm, peaceful, gentle.

The next higher type is that of Dâsya, i.e. servantship; it comes when a man thinks he is the servant of the Lord. The attachment of the faithful servant unto the master is his ideal.

The next type of love is Sakhya, friendship — "Thou art our beloved friend." Just as a man opens his heart to his friend and knows that the friend will never chide him for his faults but will always try to help him, just as there is the idea of equality between him and his friend, so equal love flows in and out between the worshipper and his friendly God. Thus God becomes our friend, the friend who is near, the friend to whom we may freely tell all the tales of our lives. The innermost secrets of our hearts we may place before Him with the great assurance of safety and support. He is the friend whom the devotee accepts as an equal. God is viewed here as our playmate. We may well say that we are all playing in this universe. Just as children play their games, just as the most glorious kings and emperors play their own games, so is the Beloved Lord Himself in sport with this universe. He is perfect; He does not want anything. Why should He create? Activity is always with us for the fulfilment of a certain want, and want always presupposes imperfection. God is perfect; He has no wants. Why should He go on with this work of an ever-active creation? What purpose has He in view? The stories about God creating this world for some end or other that we imagine are good as stories, but not otherwise. It is all really in sport; the universe is His play going on. The whole universe must after all be a big piece of pleasing fun to Him. If you are poor, enjoy that as fun; if you are rich, enjoy the fun of being rich; if dangers come, it is also good fun; if happiness comes, there is more good fun. The world is just a playground, and we are here having good fun, having a game; and God is with us playing all the while, and we are with Him playing. God is our eternal playmate. How beautifully He is playing! The play is finished when the cycle: comes to an end. There is rest for a shorter or longer time; again all come out and play. It is only when you forget that it is all play and that you are also helping in the play, it is only then that misery and sorrows come. Then the heart becomes heavy, then the world weighs upon you with tremendous power. But as soon as you give up the serious idea of reality as the characteristic of the changing incidents of the three minutes of life and know it to be but a stage on which we are playing, helping Him to play, at once misery ceases for you. He plays in every atom; He is playing when He is building up earths, and suns, and moons; He is playing with the human heart, with animals, with plants. We are His chessmen; He puts the chessmen on the board and shakes them up. He arranges us first in one way and then in another, and we are consciously or unconsciously helping in His play. And, oh, bliss! we are His playmates!

The next is what is known as Vâtsalya, loving God not as our Father but as our Child. This may look peculiar, but it is a discipline to enable us to detach all ideas of power from the concept of God. The idea of power brings with it awe. There should be no awe in love. The ideas of reverence and obedience are necessary for the formation of character; but when character is formed, when the lover has tasted the calm, peaceful love and tasted also a little of its intense madness, then he need talk no more of ethics and discipline. To conceive God as mighty, majestic, and glorious, as the Lord of the universe, or as the God of gods, the lover says he does not care. It is to avoid this association with God of the fear-creating sense of power that he worships God as his own child. The mother and the father are not moved by awe in relation to the child; they cannot have any reverence for the child. They cannot think of asking any favour from the child. The child's position is always that of the receiver, and out of love for the child the parents will give up their bodies a hundred times over. A thousand lives they will sacrifice for that one child of theirs, and, therefore, God is loved as a child. This idea of loving God as a child comes into existence and grows naturally among those religious sects which believe in the incarnation of God. For the Mohammedans it is impossible to have this idea of God as a child; they will shrink from it with a kind of horror. But the Christian and the Hindu can realise it easily, because they have the baby Jesus and the baby Krishna. The women in India often look upon themselves as Krishna's mother; Christian mothers also may take up the idea that they are Christ's mothers, and it will bring to the West the knowledge of God's Divine Motherhood which they so much need. The superstitions of awe and reverence in relation to God are deeply rooted in the bears of our hearts, and it takes long years to sink entirely in love our ideas of reverence and veneration, of awe and majesty and glory with regard to God.

There is one more human representation of the divine ideal of love. It is known as Madhura, sweet, and is the highest of all such representations. It is indeed based on the highest manifestation of love in this world, and this love is also the strongest known to man. What love shakes the whole nature of man, what love runs through every atom of his being — makes him mad, makes him forget his own nature, transforms him, makes him either a God or a demon — as the love between man and woman. In this sweet representation of divine love God is our husband. We are all women; there are no men in this world; there is but One man, and this is He, our Beloved. All that love which man gives to woman, or woman to man, has here to be given up to the Lord.

All the different kinds of love which we see in the world, and with which we are more or less playing merely, have God as the one goal; but unfortunately, man does not know the infinite ocean into which this mighty river of love is constantly flowing, and so, foolishly, he often tries to direct it to little dolls of human beings. The tremendous love for the child that is in human nature is not for the little doll of a child; if you bestow it blindly and exclusively on the child, you will suffer in consequence. But through such suffering will come the awakening by which you are sure to find out that the love which is in you, if it is given to any human being, will sooner or later bring pain and sorrow as the result. Our love must, therefore, be given to the Highest One who never dies and never changes, to Him in the ocean of whose love there is neither ebb nor flow. Love must get to its right destination, it must go unto Him who is really the infinite ocean of love. All rivers flow into the ocean. Even the drop of water coming down from the mountain side cannot stop its course after reaching a brook or a river, however big it may be; at last even that drop somehow does find its way to the ocean. God is the one goal of all our passions and emotions. If you want to be angry, be angry with Him. Chide your

Beloved, chide your Friend. Whom else can you safely chide? Mortal man will not patiently put up with your anger; there will be a reaction. If you are angry with me I am sure quickly to react, because I cannot patiently put up with your anger. Say unto the Beloved, "Why do You not come to me; why do You leave me thus alone?" Where is there any enjoyment but in Him? What enjoyment can there be in little clods of earth? It is the crystallised essence of infinite enjoyment that we have to seek, and that is in God. Let all our passions and emotions go up unto Him. They are meant for Him, for if they miss their mark and go lower, they become vile; and when they go straight to the mark, to the Lord, even the lowest of them becomes transfigured. All the energies of the human body and mind, howsoever they may express themselves, have the Lord as their one goal, as their Ekâyana. All loves and all passions of the human heart must go to God. He is the Beloved. Whom else can this heart love? He is the most beautiful, the most sublime, He is beauty itself, sublimity itself. Who in this universe is more beautiful than He? Who in this universe is more fit to become the husband than He? Who in this universe is fitter to be loved than He? So let Him be the husband, let Him be the Beloved.

Often it so happens that divine lovers who sing of this divine love accept the language of human love in all its aspects as adequate to describe it. Fools do not understand this; they never will. They look at it only with the physical eye. They do not understand the mad throes of this spiritual love. How can they? "For one kiss of Thy lips, O Beloved! One who has been kissed by Thee, has his thirst for Thee increasing for ever, all his sorrows vanish, and he forgets all things except Thee alone." Aspire after that kiss of the Beloved, that touch of His lips which makes the Bhakta mad, which makes of man a god. To him, who has been blessed with such a kiss, the whole of nature changes, worlds vanish, suns and moons die out, and the universe itself melts away into that one infinite ocean of love. That is the perfection of the madness of love

Ay, the true spiritual lover does not rest even there; even the love of husband and wife is not mad enough for him. The Bhaktas take up also the idea of illegitimate love, because it is so strong; the impropriety of it is not at all the thing they have in view. The nature if this love is such that the more obstructions there are for its free play, the more passionate it becomes. The love between husband and wife is smooth, there are no obstructions there. So the Bhaktas take up the idea of a girl who is in love with her own beloved, and her mother or father or husband objects to such love; and the more anybody obstructs the course of her love, so much the more is her love tending to grow in strength. Human language cannot describe how Krishna in the groves of Vrindâ was madly loved, how at the sound of his voice the ever-blessed Gopis rushed out to meet him, forgetting everything, forgetting this world and its ties, its duties, its joys, and its sorrows. Man, O man, you speak of divine love and at the same time are able to attend to all the vanities of this world — are you sincere? "Where Râma is, there is no room for any desire — where desire is, there is no room for Rama; these never coexist — like light and darkness they are never together."

CHAPTER X
Conclusion

When this highest ideal of love is reached, philosophy is thrown away; who will then care for it? Freedom, Salvation, Nirvâna — all are thrown away; who cares to become free while in the enjoyment of divine love? "Lord, I do not want wealth, nor friends, nor beauty, nor learning, nor even freedom; let me be born again and again, and be Thou ever my Love. Be Thou ever and ever my Love." "Who cares to become sugar?" says the Bhakta, "I want to taste sugar." Who will then desire to become free and one with God? "I may know that I am He; yet will I take myself away from Him and become different, so that I may enjoy the Beloved." That is what the Bhakta says. Love for love's sake is his highest enjoyment. Who will not be bound hand and foot a thousand times over to enjoy the Beloved? No Bhakta cares for anything except love, except to love and to be loved. His unworldly love is like the tide rushing up the river; this lover goes up the river against the current. The world calls him mad. I know one whom the world used to call mad, and this was his answer: "My friends, the whole world is a lunatic asylum. Some are mad after worldly love, some after name, some after fame, some after money, some after salvation and going to heaven. In this big lunatic asylum I am also mad, I am mad after God. If you are mad after money, I am mad after God. You are mad; so am I. I think my madness is after all the best." The true Bhakta's love is this burning madness before which everything else vanishes for him. The whole universe is to him full of love and love alone; that is how it seems to the lover. So when a man has this love in him, he becomes eternally blessed, eternally happy. This blessed madness of divine love alone can cure for ever the disease of the world that is in us. With desire, selfishness has vanished. He has drawn near to God, he has thrown off all those vain desires of which he was full before.

We all have to begin as dualists in the religion of love. God is to us a separate Being, and we feel ourselves to be separate beings also. Love then comes in the middle, and man begins to approach God, and God also comes nearer and nearer to man. Man takes up all the various relationships of life, as father, as mother, as son, as friend, as master, as lover, and projects them on his ideal of love, on his God. To him God exists as all these, and the last point of his progress is reached when he feels that he has become absolutely merged in the object of his worship. We all begin with love for ourselves, and the unfair claims of the little self make even love selfish. At last, however, comes the full blaze of light, in which this little self is seen to have become one with the Infinite. Man himself is transfigured in the presence of this Light of Love, and he realises at last the beautiful and inspiring truth that Love, the Lover, and the Beloved are One.

www.ingramcontent.com/pod-product-compliance
Lightning Source LLC
LaVergne TN
LVHW042111190726
843493LV00006B/1439